Warrior Heart, Pilgrim Soul: An Immigrant's Journey

Poems by Maria Victoria A. Grageda-Smith

Published by Pilgrim Books and
printed in the United States of America by CreateSpace,
North Charleston, SC (an Amazon company).

LCCN No. 2013904817
ISBN-13: 978-1482724301

Dedication

To my husband, Steve, and our children, Francesca and Travis, who are my constant muses; to my mother, Teresita A. Grageda, whose defiance to the end testified to her passion for a beautiful life; and to all the struggling masses of immigrant humanity who have traveled this road with me: Thank you, all, for your inspiration of eternal hope and courage.

Contents

Preface   7

Prologue
    Pilgrim I   17

Chapter 1. Journey Through Fire and Water
    Sunset on a Beach on the
        Other Side of the Pacific   19
    Journey   23
    Prejudice   24
    Pondering Upon a Poem   25
    Eve's Rhythm   27
    Sisyphus Recurring   29
    Ode to the Resting Lady   31
    Have You Seen Me Lately, Dr. Seuss?   32
    The Monster in the Kitchen   35
    Heart's Storm, Soul's Tempest   36
    Elegy for a Housewife   37

Chapter 2. Journey Through Earth and Air
    To My Muse   39
    Writer, Playing God   40
    Critics   42
    Speck of Dust   43
    Fossils in July   45
    To Vincent   46
    Painter   47
    Actor   49
    Dancer   51
    Sculptor   53
    Singer   54
    Musician   55
    Poet   56

Chapter 3. Journey Through Love

Warrior Heart   58

To the WASPy Old Gentleman
     Across the Room   59

Platonic Love   63

What If   64

Blame It on Neruda   65

Second Time Around   67

A Love Letter to My Students   69

Love's Nature   70

Chapter 4. Journey Through Family

Family   73

A Love Song for My Husband   74

A Thankful Marriage   75

Dream House Hunters   77

For My Daughter and Her Friends
     on High School's Eve   79

Valentine's Child   81

Bus Boy   82

Old Letters   83

My Mother's Hair   86

A Letter to My Mother   88

The Gardener   93

Generations   94

Midwest Winter Garden   95

To *Lola*, on Her Ninetieth Birthday   96

Reconstruction of Lost Things   98

Chapter 5. Journey Through Friendship

BFF   101

Refugee of Old Dreams   102

Requiem for a Beloved Friend   104

Kindred Souls   105

Chapter 6. Journey Through the (Human) Race

People's Poet	107
For Carson	108
Abu Graib	110
Diaspora of Luzviminda's Children	112
Valentine's Dance of the Mail-Order Bride	114
Turning a Corner	117
Rain-Fool	118
Pilgrim II	120
Rattled in Seattle	124
The Dying Season	125

Chapter 7. Journey Through the Soul

Breakthrough	127
Meditations Before a Sink Full of Dirty Dishes	128
Easter Vigil	130
Mark of Life	131
Purity of Nothingness	133
The Sleepers	134
Messenger	136
Contemplations	138
Exorcism of Childhood Saints	140
Quantum Entanglement	142
After Dust Settles	143
Memory of Water	145
These Are the Rains	147

Epilogue

Homecoming	149

Acknowledgements

Acknowledgements	151

About the Author

About the Author	155

Preface

As a Filipino immigrant writer in the United States, one question that continuously nags me during the writing process is the issue of identity.

Who am I as a writer? After procrastinating on addressing this challenge for the longest time, I could no longer avoid it the moment I decided to integrate the various poems I'd written in the past twenty years into a single collection. What is the common thread, theme, or spirit unifying these poems? What justifies presenting them as one body of work? I suspect the ultimate answer lies, at its core, in defining the poet who wrote them.

In attempting to define who I am as a writer, I find I have to start from the beginning. And my beginning is this: Like my beloved native country and people, I am, as my poem *A Letter to My Mother* (that forms part of this collection) describes:

…Always seemingly caught between worlds –
neither here nor there, neither this nor that,
eluding tidy description, belonging nowhere….

I'm astounded to realize I may be, after all, no different from the riddle within a riddle of a poem I've long rebelled against.

Do I see myself as a Filipino writer who only happens to reside in the United States? Or do I consider myself an American writer who incidentally has Philippine roots? Is the place in which I write determinative of who I am as a writer? Or is my identity determined by nationality roots, the dominant sociocultural construct that thereby becomes the frame of reference for my work?

So many questions; so many layers of nuanced issues to explore. And the possible answers, equally complex!

To start with, the fact that I write mainly in English is enough for some Filipino writers to repudiate me as an authentic Filipino writer. For to them, language is *the* medium of identity, and failure to write in one's native language is an affront to our culture, dismissing me, the suspect writer, as just another neocolonial agent.

So am I then simply an "American" writer? Which begs the question, "Who *is* the *American* writer?" While I am now a United States citizen, I doubt this is enough for me to claim that I have become an American writer. For I came to the United States at a later age, already immersed in the narrative and traditions that have shaped and inspired the literature of my native land. A writer's identity cannot be based on mere citizenship—having been born and raised in the United States, for instance, could be influential, even persuasive, but certainly not conclusive. Neither can a writer be referenced solely in terms of the location of the act of writing—thus, residing and writing within the United States territory may be irrelevant to many if the cultural lens from which one sees and tries to understand her subject matter is so far removed from the cultural lens of the country in which she lives. But from which cultural lens should an American writer adopt a perspective? Indeed, what is American culture but a kaleidoscope of many varied cultures?

It occurs to me at this point I may only have been chasing a phantom—when it seems within reach, it disappears once I try to grasp it. Perhaps being an American writer is merely an abstraction, an intangible concept, just as America itself is a conceptual ideal: a rogue nation formed by immigrants that dared rebel against a king and declared itself a government of the people, by the people, and for the people pledged to the principles of life, liberty, and the pursuit of happiness.

But more than two hundred years later, we still can't agree what American democracy and this "life, liberty, and the pursuit of happiness" principle really mean. And while I have some idea enough to ascribe and subscribe to them, this isn't all I believe in either. I also happen to admire, among others, the very "Asian" ideal of sacrificing individual welfare

—

8

(to certain limits, of course) to the larger good of the greater community of family, clan, barrio, tribe, village, and nation. Not that Americans aren't capable of subordinating individual aspirations to societal aims. It's just that compared to the American inclination, most Asian cultures tend to rank group identity and welfare above individual identity and well-being. Both persuasions — American individualism and Asian communalism — are of course double-edged swords. But this isn't my point of inquiry. With these combined albeit varying worldviews within me, I simply wonder whether it is more practical to see myself in a more general, generic, "safe" sense — say, as an "Asian American" writer, perhaps?

Seems reasonable, but many Asians would balk at the categorization of Filipinos as "Asian." And rightly so, for the Philippine native culture and world view, compared to those of our neighbors in Southeast Asia, are uniquely Western oriented, owing to four hundred years of Spanish colonial rule and fifty years of United States occupation that saw my grandparents and other forebears become Spanish-speaking Catholics and my parents educated in English-speaking classrooms.

I was born during a nationalist period in which self-styled patriots proudly embarked upon the creation of a Philippine "national" language they called "Filipino" and, upon its launching, raised a new generation of Filipinos in the two official national languages of Filipino and English. In my case, I was brought up trilingual — speaking and writing mainly in the two official languages plus Pampango, the dialect of my home province.

Later, as I pursued studies in this so-called national language called "Filipino," I realized it was essentially nothing more than Tagalog, the dialect of the capital city of the largest island in the country, an archipelago composed of more than seven thousand islands with their own regional dialects. It struck me as a rather pretentious national language, for imposing the dialect of the nation's capital on other regions of the country that had strong linguistic traditions of their own could be seen as nothing more than the perpetuation of the colonial model by so-called nationalists who, after the expulsion of our colonial masters, now forced their own cultural parameters on the subordinated regional satellites. One could thus argue that there is actually no true "Filipino" national language apart from the arbitrary investiture of the Tagalog dialect as such national language.

But that's another topic to explore in another body of work, I'm afraid. Still, one can see from this that questioning my identity as a Filipino writer just because I happen to write in English is nothing more than facetious. Writing in English does not make me any less a Filipino writer than someone who writes, for instance, in Cebuano or Ilocano (other types of Philippine dialects). Besides, whatever happened to "English" being the *other* Philippine official national language?

At this point, one might suggest that my bilingual skills in Filipino and English plus my United States citizenship and residence altogether substantiate my identification as a "Filipino American writer," plain and simple. But what does this term "Filipino American" mean, exactly? Upon closer inspection, there appears nothing plain or simple about it. Am I equally as Filipino as I am American, or am I more Filipino than American?

After two decades of residence in the United States and marriage to a native-born American who typifies the average American who can't speak any language apart from English, I tend to forget the terms used in my native tongue, tripping over the words, sometimes inventing labels that replicate those I can't momentarily recover from that part of my brain that stores the tapestry of my multilingual memory that contains names for concepts and feelings the English language has never dreamed of. Pity, for the most I seem to achieve these days after talking in my native language is just a harder accent on my "English-speak" that immediately betrays the last encounter I've had. My husband and children are quick to note this when it happens and tease me accordingly. "You've been chatting with Filipinos again, haven't you, Mom?" I am always surprised at how this hits me with a fleeting sense of guilt, as if I've committed a crime, as if employing my native tongue has somehow taken away from my powers as an English-speaking and writing creature.

While I'm not sure whether I've graduated into dreaming in English, I do know that I think, speak, and write faster and better in English than in any other language in my waking hours. But the sentiments and ruminations? As Filipino as "Pinoy spaghetti" — a Filipinized version of an American interpretation of a European dish that, if the writer who called himself Marco Polo is to be believed, was in turn inspired by the Chinese! Savor that.

And so, *Filipino American*? By all means, but only as a compromise, since I can't think of a better term to call myself. The less complicated evil, you see.

However, this far from settles the matter for me. I still believe the question of writer's identity does truly matter to one's writing. But how so? "Write what you know" is what mentors always tell the beginner writers among us. Yet if I only write what I know, how does it matter whether or not I am conscious of my cultural and national identity as a writer? Should not my identity simply follow as a matter of course from the substance of my writing, which in turn, one could reasonably assume, comes directly from what I know? Or does my consciousness of my identity as a writer subjectively and independently affect the objectivity of my writing?

So far, the best answer that presents itself to me is this: Ultimately, who I am as a writer is very much connected to my motivations for writing — an easier path of exploration for me because if there's anything I'm certain of, it's the reasons why I write. Through my writing, I aim not only to express myself but, equally important, to be heard. Thus I decided early on that my work should first and foremost be accessible to the everyday person, without succumbing to what is merely pedestrian or popular. This is what underlies the direct, raw, naked, tender, passionate — even confrontational — qualities of my poems, including the occasional tongue-in-cheek attempts at humor. Thus, my poetry exposes me to utmost vulnerability, thereby inviting my readers and listeners into a covenant of intimate trust with me. Nonetheless, while actual events and persons inspire most of my poems, the reader should not make the mistake of assuming that my poetry is entirely biographical, for the storyteller in me often utilizes the dramatization afforded by the fictional dream in order to draw out a poem's universal significance.

Indeed, I strive for poetry and fiction that celebrate not only the unique but universal in human experience, that are not content to explore the singular perspective but dare touch the nerve of the general human condition. I am especially inspired by the transcendence and humanity of Filipino writer Dr. José Rizal, American poet Walt Whitman, and Chilean poet Pablo Neruda; the contemporary voices of Ted Hooser, Billy Collins, and Charles Wright; the timelessness of William Butler Yeats and T. S. Eliot; the romantic effluence of Emily Dickinson, Elizabeth Barrett Browning, and Edna St. Vincent Millay; the lyrical affluence of Persian poets Omar Khayyam and Melvana Jalal ad-Din Muhammad Rumi, including Lebanese American Khalil Gibran; the dual voice of exprobration and bold sensuality of the ancient biblical psalmists; and last, but not least, the refreshing, childlike innocence, honesty, and simplicity of Theodor Seuss Geisel, fondly known as Dr. Seuss. I try to cull these varied voices together to work and blend them in assisting me to achieve a uniquely eclectic yet universal literary style.

Unfortunately, interest in contemporary poetry doesn't appear to be quite universal particularly in the United States where patronage seems patchy apart from the small, elitist following cultivated by the arguably nepotistic system between MFA students, graduates, and professors, on the one hand, and their university presses and allied literary journals, on the other. Only a few brave souls from within the hallowed halls of that privileged circle have mustered the humility to boldly acknowledge there is even a problem in that.

Stop a man on the street and ask what poetry he has heard or read lately, and I'm going to bet he will look at you as if you were crazy. Compare this with the grassroots patronage in its time of ancient or classical poetry that drew its inspiration from the frustrations and ecstasies of common people going about their common lives glorified in songs sung by the bards and troubadours who lived among them. The work of those early poets did not just describe but celebrated and uplifted the human soul.

In contrast, reading the kind of poetry favored by many ivory tower publications today is like wading through a riddle within a riddle so that one wonders whether the poet indeed wanted to connect with a real audience or was only enamored with the sound of his intellect verbalizing itself. In the end, this makes those of us who expect more from poetry beg the question, "What was the point of it all?" We are underwhelmed by the supposed substance misrepresented by the highbrow tone and style of the composition, and then overwhelmed with the residual feeling of having been taken for a ride, misled into thinking there was more to it than there really was, an experience not unlike perhaps of the disenchanted subjects of the monarch in the story of *The Emperor's New Clothes*. From the start, I knew this was not the kind of poetry I wanted to write, for it is a luxury I cannot afford as I yearn to identify and be identified with the greater masses of otherwise would-be poetry enthusiasts who feel let down and abandoned by many poets of their time.

Like everything that aspires to greatness, poetry and fiction have the power to allow us a glimpse of the best and worst versions of ourselves. In exploring the freedoms afforded by this immense power, I am guided by a couple of principles. In fiction, for example, a writer is urged to depict how his character has evolved by the end of the story. I find this a useful tool in poetry as well, save in this case, it is the reader or listener who, I hope, is moved, if not changed, by the experience. In addition, I challenge myself to write poems that suggest a glimmer of hope, no matter how faint, to sustain the reader's and, perhaps more importantly, my own faith in human nature. In so doing, I know I am opening my work to criticisms of being "oversentimental" by those who worship detachment as the ideal standard of writing discipline and aesthetic, if not literary merit.

This does not daunt me. For I refuse to be the "literary orphan" lamented by David Foster Wallace as seen from this passage from his monumental novel, *Infinite Jest*:

"Postmodern irony and cynicism's become an end in itself, a measure of hip sophistication and literary savvy. Few artists dare to try to talk about ways of working toward redeeming what's wrong, because they'll look sentimental and naive to all the weary ironists. Irony's gone from liberating to enslaving…. The postmodern founders' patricidal work was great, but patricide produces orphans, and no amount of revelry can make up for the fact that writers my age have been literary orphans throughout our formative years."

To me, the ultimate value of poetry and fiction lies not in the exposition of the existential human condition but in facilitating man's search for meaning. In this regard, Victor E. Frankl's book *Man's Search For Meaning* shows its lasting impression on me. At the core of the theory of logotherapy that Frankl expounds in his book is the belief that man's primary motivational force is his search for meaning, that man can withstand anything as long as he can somehow assign some value or significance to his experience. This is especially crucial for the immigrant's experience.

All over the world, people in all walks of life continue to struggle to make sense of their lives—that age-old question—especially those driven from their homes and native countries in search of a better life. Having lost the anchor of their homeland and along with that much of what is familiar and dear to them, immigrants struggle to re-create and redefine their individual and social identities in their new environments, sometimes in the face of much persecution and discrimination. Their struggle is compounded by the immediate material necessity of establishing viable means of livelihood to provide for themselves and their families — literally to keep body and soul together. It is in the midst of such great suffering that many might question the purpose of their struggle, until they are reminded of the soulful aspect of their exile: their desire to support their loved ones, many of whom are still back home in the old country desperately relying on them for their most basic necessities.

It is in moments similar to these dark nights of the soul that I rediscover the enduring power of poetry to soothe, heal, and enlighten. The literary masterpieces I enjoy most in this regard are those of writers and poets who seem to have succeeded in decoding some aspect of the great mystery of life and left their work as maps to help us navigate a meaningful path to a way of living and being that aims far beyond mere existence.

I hope my readers can glean their own insights from the shared human experience they might decipher from my personal journey, as witnessed by this collection of poems.

Maria Victoria A. Grageda-Smith
October 2013

Prologue

Pilgrim I

From across the seas I came,
        out of the Land of the Orient Pearl,
To this "Land of Immigrants," they say;
        yet seeking not its comforts
More than union with my Beloved.

I am in limbo among loyalties fading,
Identity hovering 'midst
        the misty recollections of the soul,
And I find: I am among the first
        of many yet to become.

I feel beholden not to any sovereign,
        save none but humanity itself.
I am a citizen of the world,
        a child of humankind:
Do they not recognize their own?

When will they wake up to the truth — that
people are no longer to be separated:
        by time or space,
        by color or creed,
        by laws or jurisdictions?

The divisions among us
        are illusory as darkness,
And we continue to walk the earth
        as wandering strangers,
Till we find ourselves home
        at each other's hearth.

Chapter 1. Journey Through Fire and Water

Sunset on a Beach on the
Other Side of the Pacific

So is this where it all again begins for me?

On a beach on the other side of the Pacific,
watching the sun lower itself into a bath of frigid
waters, grabbing me with bleached fingers of

spray and foam, surrounding, engulfing, burying
brown feet in white sand, as if planting my body
irrevocably in this strange new land before my soul

has had the chance to renege, before it's ready
to say good-bye to the Motherland across the sea?
Is this how the immigrant journeys in this country —

the corpus arriving, while spirit still dreams of the
landscape of its birth that, left behind, assumes
at once the martyred hero's legacy — larger, more

beautiful, and more noble than it really is? Like a
period movie in sepia — tinting everything with rosy
film of romantic delusion, suppressing odious sight,

like the whitewashed walls the Madam built to conceal
the slums of her city with its putrid pots of bubbling,
seething discontent and ignorance pressing against

the pink marble palaces of the maggots who live off of
the living dead — yes, that stone fit for the gods, quarried
in rural blight by skilled masons who can't afford even

a paltry tin roof to shelter their sons' heads. And the
stink camouflaged with Chanel No. 5! God, yes, the

stink of open sewers flowing like rivers of excrement

across the city, and the muddied waters that turn into
floods each typhoon season like the expired parting of
the Red Sea released by the broken walls of Jericho

upon the cracked banks of aqueous memory now lost
through death of the old forests whose corpses line
the libraries of the ivory towers of the learned, and

the cocktail bars of Hollywood, and the cigar-smoking
salons of Wall Street. They haunt me still — those images
of raging floodwaters, where carcasses of mad, stray dogs

and malnourished *carabaos* bob up and down, side by side
with gelatinous remains of infants snatched away from
their mothers' breasts, emptied now of their milk, sucked

dry by philandering, jobless, beer-drunk husbands raping
both their land and women as sorry revenge for their own
castrations: the castration of a people now scattered on the

earth in a diaspora they liken to what happened to those
who call themselves the Chosen Ones. No wonder they
sing the lamentations of the ancient psalmists as if

these songs were their own. For they have nothing left
of theirs. What little they had — even this had been taken
from them: They who drug themselves with their religion

and then call it faith, who have become an invisible people.
For they have given up their children to the pedophiles
of the world; their mothers to the children of mothers unfit

to mother their own; and their fathers to the scorching
deserts of the sickle moon, harvesting the black gold

for the veiled lords tending fields of terror in Mindanao—

that eternal battleground of Cross and Crescent riding
on the winds of the unrepentant war now reaching
these shores in currents laced with blood and ash,

while my feet wallow in pools of orphaned melancholy
of paradise lost. Is there nowhere to run, nowhere to hide
from this fate? Till I realize: It's the same ocean after all—

these waters that lap in throbbing agony against my feet.
How I'd love to be the gilded crimson sphere sinking
upon the singed waters, poached clean of old wounds!

It beckons—this new old sun retiring from the day,
surrendering its splendor to the night—there, where
the horizon unites Apollo and Diana in matrimonial

dance each day, whose silver lining barely registers
in my mind's eye. For I remember the sun setting over
Manila Bay as more glorious than this new old sun

eyeing me like Narcissus desperately seeking his lover.
Never mind if the divine glow of the sunset on the other
side of the Pacific derives more from illusion of light

diffused by pollution. I am Proserpina, surrendering
myself to the unknown, while dreaming of spring
in the land of eternal summers the mermaids call

Pearl of the Orient Seas. And I remember how the warm
waters on those volcanic shores have birthed luminous
white pearls from the vexing black sands of hopelessness—

as big and radiant and lustrous as the full moon over
California, and how the spirit that bred those gems

of affliction is the same spirit that churns the blood

that still runs in my veins. So I plant myself firmly in this
strange new land I now call my own, cutting flesh against
sea-rock in a bloodletting ritual that marries my heritage

with my Beloved's, baptizing this land with the joys and
sorrows and dreams of my people who are creating new
beginnings from scraps that fall off of their masters' tables,

washing ourselves clean of our real and imagined sins,
stripping our souls bare with flagellations flung by the
crashing waves of destiny. Now shall I serenade this

landscape with the songs of my Motherland, joining
in the symphony of other voices carried upon these
shores by tides of change.

Do you hear the dolphins singing the Chumash song?

Journey

The bus revs up, taking me
away from where I've been.

The world rushes around me: cars, trucks, joggers,
cyclists, mothers with strollers, dogs with owners.
Everyone seems to be going somewhere.

Even nature is complicit: birds fly away, leaves
dance with the wind, grass shimmers and sways,
squirrels skitter, climbing towers of dominion.

I am the lone still life in this moving landscape.
I, alone, remain—an outsider, looking in.

Prejudice

I cannot fathom your resolve
to keep away
from flesh and blood.

Could it be that
your fear is greater than your hope;
your pride greater than your love;
your hatred for their mother, a bottomless pit?

If so, I pity you then.
For we shall not pass
your way again.

I shall charge the wheels of Fate
to rip the loom of karmic cycle.

So I and my children,
and my children's children
shall not have to bear
the cold delusions
of your small mind,
made smaller by your persistence
in your ignorance,
your constant need to occupy our universe
with your wounds.

And we shall finally be free
of your prejudice,
your toxic shadow,
your unbearably common heart.

You've no idea what you're missing.
Or perhaps you do. And still.

Pondering Upon a Poem

I cannot ponder upon your poem, for you speak
too much the language of the mind
and I, the heart.

I cannot ponder upon your poem,
for you fly to heights of abstraction
and hide behind clouds of obscurity,
and then you lose me.

I cannot ponder upon your poem,
for you rant and rave,
shout and break
the silence necessary
to understanding.

Most of all, I cannot ponder upon your poem
because the breadth and depth of your love
isn't wide enough, nor deep enough
to embrace both your self and me.

Look at me with the eyes of your soul
and tell me: Do you see me at all?
Can you tell we are bound to each
other, as flesh is to dust?

That my experience isn't less special
because it isn't as earth-shaking like yours?
That my way of life isn't as marginal as
you think it might be, and therefore
no less worthy to explore?
That I am no less human because
you don't see a tear in my eye?

And because I don't rant and rave,
nor shout and scream,
nor throw and break,
nor stomp and hit,
nor fight and take flight
to a world where you seek
to be understood,
yet refuse to understand
that you and I:
we are ultimately,
hopelessly —
One.

Eve's Rhythm

It starts with
pinching pain on belly's
side, pulled by aching undertow,
heavy on the gut, spreading
to groin and
thigh.

Stabbing twinge
on bosom raw, then
throbbing migraine: that creeping,
treacherous thief of time;
that saboteur of
productivity.

Happy one day,
miserable, next. Life changes
overnight. Misdemeanors inflate
into capital sins. Temper
rises like tsunami
winds.

Crimson tide swells,
inundating womb with
pulsating cramp. Burning soreness
at pelvic core, expelling
lapsed, inchoate
life.

Sole escape is
nine months' incubation
of wretched agony that surpasses
all. Then post-natal
depression seals
infamy.

Thirty more years of this, and
the cycle begins again:
this time barrenness
signaled by hot
flashes.

Price of Adam passing the buck.

Sisyphus Recurring

I'm tired.

Tired of carrying the weight of my life.
Tired of carrying this body around,
lugging it from floor to floor,
on stairs that go nowhere —
whether up or down,
no one really knows.

And for what?

Tired of doing good and not doing good.
Tired of working hard and not tasting
the fruits of my labors. Tired of cleaning —
it never ends! The dirt always follows me
around like a nagging dust devil saying,
"I'm not done with you yet."

For Chris'sakes! Enough already.

Enough with all the coming and going, dressing
and undressing, talking and not talking, eating
and not eating, pleasing and displeasing, making
love and making war, winning and losing,
building and destroying, birthing and killing,
and then sleeping, only to wake up —
to get tired, all over again.

Enough of kidding myself with,
"There's more to life than this."
Of searching for meaning where
there's none. Of crying like a voice
in the wilderness, hoping someone
will hear or, better yet, answer.

This is it.
Is there nothing else?

Enough of dreaming.
Time to wake up:

To get tired —
all over again.

Excuse me
while I breathe.

Ode to the Resting Lady
(At the Chicago Museum of Art)

"Resting" your maker named you.
>Yet there's nothing restful in your pose.
Your naked breast marks your heart—
>its beating pounds in my ears.

Your pale face turns toward the light—
>tell me, is it to eastern or western sun?
What troubled thoughts brew behind those eyes—
>percolating grudge or bitter devise?

See:
>you're no different from me—
Woman:
>restless against your fate.

Have You Seen Me Lately, Dr. Seuss?

I think I'm missing something.
I'm not sure what—or how.
I'm certain it's important,
I've got to find it now.

Between the sheets, under the
pillows, I look for it;
Out the door, through the
hallway, on the floor.

Up the stairs,
down the stairs;
perhaps the basement,
the garage, somewhere?

Beneath the cushions,
under the couch;
behind the drapes,
a scorpion—watch out!

Above the door frame,
below the mat;
feeling the underside
of the old flowerpot.

It occurs to me,
I might look in the car;
for the last time I saw it,
it was passing me by.

Then again,
I could be wrong,
for now I see,
it's all gone.

Why, I could swear,
just yesterday —
'twas standing before me,
face to face!

Just one last look —
for heaven's sake!
This always happens
when I am late!

Got to hurry —
it should be here.
One mustn't be tardy
when destiny's near.

As luck would have it,
I come up short;
I arrive complete —
less what I've lost.

Sadly, I return
to where it all began,
and wouldn't you know it —
there it is again!

I look at it closely
to check I have it right;
but what stares back at me
gives me a fright!

An impostor, a drifter,
someone who looks like me!
But goodness, gracious —
is it she or is it me?

Who is faking whom,

I demand to know now!
If she doesn't answer soon,
there's going to be a row!

Alas, I discover,
as I face the looking glass,
I am but the shadow
of the woman that I was.

Now I know what I'm missing:
I have been missing *me*!
The dreamer, the lover —
the person I used to be.

The Monster in the Kitchen

It stared at her from across her kitchen —
that monster of stainless steel and china,
full of baked grease and dried sauces:
dregs of battles at the dinner table.

She doesn't know when she first felt it:
this knowledge of the unspoken.
She just knew it was there — like a worm
in her heart slowly eating, till only
her ghost was there: pale vision
of youthful dreams.

She stares at raisin fingers — watching
the lights play on her ring: symbol
of eternal vows given, eternal
as dirty dishes in the sink.

She weeps as one weeps for a lover lost.
How fragile love is! When spent, emotions
align with the light of recognition,
and the soul cries out for relief.

How many degrees of death has a marriage?
No one knows, save the bereaved. The changes
come in tiny drops poured into the soul,
invisible to the eye, until they spill.

What must I do to reclaim what's mine?
"Give me an offering," growled the monster.
With a flick of a switch, metal grated
upon metal, devouring the lights
off of her finger.

Heart's Storm, Soul's Tempest

Pain pours like rain in
     torrents bursting through tears,
Like thousands of little spades
     through my heart they pierce.

My mute cries of protest blast through
     thunder, beating, drumming,
Spewing fires of passion in
     blinding fury of lightning, rebelling.

In this madness that shrieks and groans,
     like the howling wind, it moans.
As heavens race monsters of black and blue,
     indigo and purple serpents fight the golden hues.
Forever, for a moment, a silver lining hides
     behind the dark, bloody reds of wounded skies.

In this ungodly hour, the splendor of heaven
     reflects only the torments of hell,
As the shattered crystal dreams of my heart
     crash into the silence —
Where despair gives way to numbness,
     devoid of feeling, save that of emptiness.

All is done:
It is finished.

Elegy for a Housewife

When I am gone —
      no songs shall be sung,
      no passionate speech shall extol
      this solitary life
      lived for others,
      buried and forgotten
      by all.

Chapter 2. Journey Through Earth and Air

To My Muse

Oh calm sublime,
      oh sacred time:
How elusive you are
      to this mortal scribe!

Might you appoint your
      charms to bless,
this creator-soul's
      restlessness?

Writer, Playing God

here I am chasing dreams
with fingertips possessed

tapping away like a madwoman
on the electronic Ouija board

the alphabets they summon
unite

in secret codes
cloning

the stories of voices
haunting

till letters become
words

and words become creatures
dancing

on my computer
screen

here, they breathe their first
breath of life

then become a thousand and one
versions of myself

living lives apart
from my own

truly in the beginning was
the word

Critics

What can I say that no one else has already said?
All the stories, songs, and poems have already
      been sung and told.
It's hard to be original nowadays.
So if anyone claims to be —
      don't believe him readily.
There are many liars in this world.

Word warlocks would give us formulae to summon
      feelings, as if on cue.
As if they've mapped the whole range of human emotions —
      all tagged, labeled, classified.
So that words, by coded placements,
      would seize us with enchantment of recognition —
Yes, this, at last, is true!

Dare I say I've hoarded melodies and fabrications
      that've escaped the scrutiny of the wicked?

Hardly do I claim this, and here they are already:
      picking on my words with pens poised like daggers,
      certain they are separating chaff from grain,
      aborting a poor harvest,
      hacking at the grains of my truth.

Silly people.
Don't they know you can't cut raw grains of rice
      with dull knives?

Speck of Dust

I'm floating between what came
before me and what comes after me.
I'm but a speck of dust
whipped up by the wind,
occupying the spaces between —
if there are still any.

I look for greatness in myself,
and find only ambition for it.
I am nothing,
yet I am everything.

When they finally hear my songs,
I will have long gone
and sought the comfort of the earth —
returned to it,
as dust is to dust.

My labors will shine their glory
on those who least deserve it,
and I shudder at the mockery of my dreams
by those whom I rebuked in this life.

Thus I prayed to my Muse:
O, Source of All Creation, grant
this humble mortal this one wish:
To create that masterpiece of
which only you are inspiration.
Grant in my lifetime what few are given:
Blessed gift of witness
to love's labors won.

I did not hear my Muse answer, then.
Only silence echoed and slithered

around me, driving me deeper into the
shadows that smother the exiled lover.

When my Muse spoke at last,
it was only through a dream
veiling my vision of her.

And she said:
If you seek only the glory of mortals,
then you shall live their hell.
But if you can find heaven in every word
you write, then you need not the glory you seek;
it has already been given you.

The few words come at last—
tentative, shy.
They are coaxed, one by one,
and arrive—wary,
but not before
I empty myself
of myself,
drop by drop,
freeing space
for my Beloved
to inhabit.

Fossils in July

New moon rising in the east,
July night air — thick and slow and hot as lava,
you could drown and burn in it.

Insects flying from everywhere in the dark,
attacking the lamp, as if to punish
the light for the sun's sins.

They say we're in the midst of another
ecological mass extinction.

I don't know my place in this, save
to savor the fate of all that live:

Here today; tomorrow, not.

And in between, I write these lines
some may read; some, not.

Like fossils-in-progress, my words fly
like moth to flame toward the burning night,
leaving ghostly imprints upon baked mud.

To Vincent

Your burning gaze shames us: we, who
      are stripped bare by the purity of your pain.
Your torment haunts us across time—
      we don't see the color of our souls
      in the brushstrokes of our lives.

You are conscience screaming,
      tearing at straitjacket.
You are lover pining, dying
      from unrequited love.

I can't bear to look at you anymore, Vincent.
Thus I bury my eyes in sunflower fields.

Painter
(For Nicole and the Masters of the Louvre)

She is master of light,
hunter of pigments of the sun.
Her hand is dancer on canvas,
jump-gliding to mad motion
of creation—mimicking life,
nature, emotion—in brushstrokes
that scream at the soul.

There are tiny dots whose meaning
can only be gleaned from afar;
sweeping strokes that tell their secrets
only when one stops long enough to
listen, and pastel palettes that hide
the dark stories behind them.

We are but merchants of the canvases
of our lives, but she is
the interpreter of dreams.

How wondrous it is that light can speak
in these tones. How heavenly design
can be revealed in a riot of color.
Oh, the teals and crimsons!
The siennas and cobalts!
The saffrons and chartreuses!
And the ever-present grays and indigos
that allow the others to shine.
How dare she capture immortality
in paltry paint and fabric!

I tell you:
She is not of this world!

How could she be?
That she could summon light from shadow,
shadow from light?

Wasn't it the Ancient One who said,
"Let there be Light," and there it was?
I plant myself on my feet as my eyes
feast on the banquet she's prepared
of fruitful harvest and luminous wine;
Reubenesque maidens unashamed of
their sex; petty aristocrats hiding behind
gems; regal plebes working the fields
herding sheep in pastoral landscape
evoking incorrupt, idyllic home; the
occasional artist with the soulful eyes
staring at us, asking, "Do you see me now?"

A feast that isn't consumed by mortal hunger,
save by immortal light from which it was born—
that invisible thief riding the wheels of time,
that enemy of the archives of history,
that will soon reclaim everything
for the shadows.

Nothing is eternal after all.
All is passing and fading from the light,
into the darkness that swallows all color,
returning it to the womb of the
Creator of creators.

Actor

Man of a Thousand Faces they called him;
I wonder if he also had a thousand feelings
to go with them — or was he merely a
master of disguise?

Did his heart wear a mask — made him laugh
when he should have cried; smiled
when he should have frowned; cursed
when he loved completely,
though foolishly?

He wore the faces of all men,
and for a few cents an hour,
also bore their burdens for them.
And they adored him. For they saw
themselves in him and made him
an icon of an era.

He showed them what a man could do
to adapt to this world. And they sang
songs to resilient human spirit after that.
They wept when he died with their
memories of themselves.

All actors since — they wear
many faces too. Mostly the mask
of happiness — urging the audience
to do the same: *To smile though
your heart is breaking.* Isn't that
the way the song goes?

How many faces do we wear each day?
Which one are you wearing now?
We've become a nation of entertainers —

amusing ourselves with our selves,
never knowing which face is real,
which face is false. The show must
go on, after all, no matter what
goes on backstage.

We've desensitized ourselves
by sensationalizing the trivial.
We've even invented games for that,
and made ourselves millionaires
for knowing little facts of little value
to the larger picture of living.

We've become a guessing nation,
gambling on the chance that
behind some mask is the true
Man of a Thousand Faces.
To remind us of who we are.
So we can throw our burdens
upon him once more.

We've always needed scapegoats for
our baggage, a sacrifice to the altar
of our egos. We hate ourselves so
much we have to kill ourselves
through another.

And that's why we had to have
the Christ.

Wasn't he the original Lon Chaney?

Dancer

She rides the air like an angel defying space and gravity,
speaking the language of the soul
mere words are clumsy
to declare.

I watch her as the light captures the tiniest movement
of a finger, the flutter of wings through arms
that rise like a phoenix from
ashen shadows.

And I am mesmerized.

Her legs are graceful visions of a white mare's sturdy
stilts, lifting and pivoting, jumping and gliding,
floating in the warm waters of fetal memory,
before all was lost to cynical mind
masquerading as sophistication —
a hollow bell clanging
its loveless tune.

And I weep.

I weep for the loss of dance in our world,
for the many still stuck and frozen
in lives of quiet desperation.

We have lost ourselves
because we have lost our dreams.
We bartered them with all that glitters,
only to find our tears have allowed
rust to sneak in the night.
It buried our brilliance in the
depths of our misery.

We haven't learned.

History repeats itself
in eternal dance of self-destruction.
We have become mere shadow dancers
chained to the strings of the Black Puppeteer—
that demon of our soul that refuses to set us free
from the frenzied dance that sucks the life
out of us, until we are but ghosts
floating in the mists
of Arcadia.

When does it end?

Meantime, we can only view this angelic apparition,
reminding us of what we were, what could have been,
and the dreams that remain forgotten
until we can pirouette back
into the arms of
Ourselves.

Sculptor

He walks the shores for corpses
of trees seasoned by time, stripped
bare by salty fingers of the ocean baring
ghosts of limbs, branches and trunks
whispering their true shapes
to him.

He gathers them like lost children
crying "Pick me! Pick me!" desperate
to live again as dancers and lovers, deer
and dolphins, and eagles that crave to soar
toward the light from the shadows
of his mind.

His hands are delirious hands of a lover:
caressing and coaxing, pushing and pulling,
chipping away at the walls that imprison
the heart that throbs deep in the wood,
until it sings.

Elsewhere, kindred spirits work
their magic on clay, stone and metal.
Their hands are refinisher's fire birthing
forms which, till then, only existed
in the womb of the soul, shaping,
molding, polishing raw contortion
into the fluid lines of
Perfection.

Singer

There's a roaring giant lodged in her throat,
a nightingale serenading the moon;
a lover swooning with passion,
or a madwoman headed for doom.

She could take you to pinnacles of joy,
inspire visions of heavenly realm,
coast you along jazzy blues,
or pull you down to depths of hell.

What magnificent instrument this is —
the human voice!
And how amazing —
the shapes it takes:

One is
petite, curvy, and bodacious;
another —
tall, slim, and straight.

It comes in different sizes —
from a princess to a pea,
and in seasons:
aged and mellow, like fine wine,
or new, like perky bubbly.

There are those born to sing in Carnegie Hall,
and those meant only for the shower stall;
yet in every case, even the angels weep,
when the singer sings with heart and soul.

Musician

The mute one sings with his fingers,
    aided by string, wood, metal, and air.
His body makes love to the music
    and they become one — the instrument and he.

It's a labor of love, no less,
    spending hours of practice
to play for a handful of audience
    who'd rather be somewhere else.

For they're attuned to the noise of the age,
    deaf to the music of the ages.
They don't care for dead men's songs —
    this language is alien to them.

They're strangers to all that requires them
    to pause from their busy lives —
to feel, think, ponder, and discover
    that their soulful rhythms

have gone away,
    left for another land
where dead men still play their music
    to the gods who listen to them.

Poet

a poet is the scorned lover of her time
weaving songs in the wind no one hears
to whom polite society feels obliged to lend
an ear and say *that's nice* as they hurry on where to
not even they know for they didn't listen if only they did
they would know what they seek is right under their noses
begging to be seen begging to be heard begging to be
embraced but they're too busy with their treasure
hunt for stone paper metal that weighs down
the soul now sinking to the bottom of the sea
where their cries can only be heard
by the poet they ignored sitting
on the crevices of time singing
sad songs to the wind
only the dead
now hear

Chapter 3. Journey Through Love

Warrior Heart

Why be ashamed of your love, my Love?
Why timid in showing courage?
Has not my passion filled your cup,
worthy of loyalty's merit?

The warmth of my lips you enjoy at will,
why turn from the fire of their truth?
Does your love only last in the heat of the night,
to melt in the heat of day's disputes?

My lover's heart is a warrior's heart,
I make no apologies for this.
Will you forsake the beauty of the rose,
for fear of the thorns that embrace it?

My soul is a young soul: ungentle and fierce!
Its burdens are beauty and truth.
I promise you no life of tranquility,
but a life lived best to the full!

Can you say to the wild beast: be still and be tamed?
Or the bird, forget dreams of flight?
Neither can you stay the tide of one's passions —
death is dearer than a life of lies.

Come then, my Love —
let's drink of life till we're drunk!
Be timid no more, but bold and brave —
let's carve our hearts on the face of the earth!

To the WASPy Old Gentleman
Across the Room

I saw
you as soon as I entered the restaurant.
for a passing moment I thought
you looked at me too.
I've never been attracted to a man
like you. I must be crazy!
You must be twenty years
older than me, or so I thought,
from the gloriously silver
yet full tuft of sleekly combed
(and pomaded?) hair on your head.
I must be getting old.

I sat
on a chair facing where you
were, so that if you wished it,
you might see me too.
But you were mindless
of my presence there — in
the midst of your baby
boomer friends.

From the distance,
between what I might touch
but could only see —

I observed
the fair complexion on your face
caressed with lines that blessed
you with wisdom's mark.

I noted

the perfectly proportioned
eyes, nose, and mouth—oh yes!
That mouth with the thin pink lips
that devoured the sandwich you so tenderly
yet eagerly bit into, mouthful by mouthful.
And I imagined myself the sandwich: soft, brown
yielding flesh wrapped around delicious,
edible secrets.

I turned
faint at the thought,
yet collected myself
for imaginings of the life
we could have shared,
and still might share—
if only you could see me.

I noticed
your long, slender fingers
and noted you didn't have a ring
on *that* finger. What foolish woman
has forsaken you? Here I am,
I know your true treasure!

In the span of time from when I ordered
my obscenely expensive gourmet pizza
until it arrived—

I imagined
you when you were a sunshine boy: sweet and precious;
a heartthrob of a teenager: tentative yet charming;
a gorgeous young man: eager for life and love;
and now: the sexy, seasoned, lonely man you are.

Oh, would that you had met me too,

in my prime, when older men like you
sought me out as a prize. But they had nothing
else to give after that, only their empty souls,
and their imagined nocturnal prowess.

Yet there you were —
on the other side of my world,
giving the best years of your life
to some bimbo who only wanted
you as *her* prize.

And so here we are today —
in the same room, yet still on different
sides of the world. Have the scabs
on your wounds scarred your heart
into forgetting, so now you give up
completely on the love of your life?
Here I am, yet you pass me by,
unknowingly.

I want
to tug at your sleeve as you walk
right by me, dismissive of the love
we could have shared and still
could share.

I breathe
in deeply the air you scented
in my space, hoping my exhaled
breath brings me back to you,
to awaken you gently into recognition,
calling you forth from the depths
of your apathy, saying,
"Return to me, my Love!"

But you walk on by,
as my husband hands me
my buttered piece of toast,
and our toddler screams
for it.

Platonic Love

This love of mine seeks only to give,
         not to take.
The loves of our lives need not fear:
         our promises remain safe.

If you'll let me, I'll share in your joys and pain,
         blessing you only with happiness.
And if, in your quiet moments, you have a kind
         thought for me, surrender it to the realm
         beyond words, and there, leave it be.

Pour only with your eyes the affections
         reserved for the honorable.
For in this world of illusions, the dispossessed
         labor under delusions of possessive
         love, tainting hearts of integrity.
They see malice where truth and beauty only aspire
         for absolute love and friendship that inspire
         a communion of souls in a world beyond flesh.

There are soul mates beyond soul mates.
This one is ours.

What If

What if
> the sun never set,
>> having never risen — tomorrow;
> the wind never blew,
>> having never reached speed;
> the flowers never bloomed,
>> having been nipped in the bud;
> the birds never flew,
>> having been clipped in the wing?

What if
> God is a figment of our imagination;
> and love is not enough;
> and time does not heal all wounds?

I shall be grateful, nonetheless,
> for this moment,
For in this moment,
> I have me and you.

Blame It on Neruda

You looked into my soul,
and I looked back.
In this world where many
stare blankly past each other,
you dared peer inside of me.
So I peered in, too.

What are we but wandering
souls searching for another
to reflect us? How many
encounters till there's finally
one who stops long enough
to be quiet, allowing ripples
upon the surface of spirit to
settle into smooth perfection
of still waters, until they're
a mirror unto us?

Loneliness is not finding
those still waters.

In my joy, I serenaded you
with Neruda. But my dead lover's
words were too much for you:
Moved you with their power.
Scared you with their passion.
Grazed you with their truth.
Made you blink.
Brought the rain to pour
upon the windows
of your soul, creating ripples
once again on the smooth
perfection of your stillness
till I could no longer see

myself in you.

Neruda shamed you
with your nakedness.
So I am, once again,
alone in mine.
Yet unashamed.
Now back to looking for
the dreamers who are awake.

Sleep tight, my love,
and dream of me,
waking you with
Neruda's reveille.

Second Time Around

Sometimes I wish we knew
and loved each other
when we were young —
at beauty's prime;

when we believed in our dreams —
our hearts, whole;
when we were fearless —
our souls, pure.

How I'd have wrapped myself
around you like wisteria to a tree,
till my vines were indistinct
from your branches.

How I'd have showered you with
blossoms, perfumed you with song,
drunk from your roots, till my roots
were inseparable from yours.

But where would we be now,
if we had each other then,
the fire of passion squandered
by youth's folly,

our light swallowed by our flames,
and we tripped, dropped our torch
in the pit of history where absolute
ideals sink in oblivion,

remembered only by those who
languish, pining for rose-colored
yesterdays that've never really been?

I'd rather have you now,
in the pit of our present slow-burning
stove of wrinkled existence,
wrapped in folds of comfort calories
and crow's feet, if it's

your parchment hand I feel
as I reach across the couch
that smells like an old dog,
and see log fires burning
on the clear surface
of your reading glasses.

A Love Letter to My Students

This precious time, this sacred moment,
this passing piece of eternity slows down
enough for me to see you and find perfection
in your ignorance: Innocence teetering between
cynicism and hope — where have all your dreams gone?

Shall I pick at the scabs of your wounds,
trace the lines of your scars, till you break out
of bland indifference — your hunger and fears
masquerading as cool sophistication?

Till you cry and lash out at me; go ahead, let it be:
I am your sacrifice at the altar of your apathy.

Till my fire melts your leaden idols,
your steel armor, your hearts of stone.

For it is in broken hearts, Dearest,
that we discover pieces of our dreams.

Here, let my blood be the glue
to paste yours back
together again.

Love's Nature

Love is indivisible, gentle,
forgiving, always giving.

Like the magnanimous sea,
it is immutable,
incapable of dilution,
although it branches off
into different rivers.

Love is omnipresent—
able to be present
to everyone it blesses,
at the same time, every time.

It's corrupt nearsightedness
that fails to see Love for what it is,
for our narrow minds and hearts fail
to fathom its sacred mysteries.

If this world were perfect, we would
welcome Love wherever it decides
to rest. It does no good to restrict it,
bottle it, nor dispense it with miserly will.

Like water, it seeps through the cracks
of our human foibles, filling the spaces
between: God is in the broken
details of our lives.

Because we lack, we aim to possess;
because we haven't found,
we aim to dispossess others
of that which we yearn for ourselves.

Don't we see — that which we seek
has been here all along? Isn't this
what is meant by the Kingdom of God
being here, right now?

May Love cure us of our deafness
to its sweet calling song,
of our self-inflicted blindness
to her colorful canvas painted
with the landscapes of our lives.

So beautiful.
So perfect.
So irrepressible.

Chapter 4. Journey Through Family

Family

I bless you,
and you bless me:
this is as it should be.

Families aren't made
by accident of birth,
but by designs of the heart.

Were we transient passengers
in this journey, it would suffice
that we travel as ships merely passing

in the night, yet we're a symphony
of souls — an orchestra of heartstrings
colliding in perfect harmony,

playing the music of the gods.

A Love Song for My Husband

He sleeps beside me: my Beloved.
His chest rises and falls to the music of his breathing.
The years have given, and they have taken—
yet still, he lies beside me.

He is man and child, all at once;
friend and foe, all at once;
lover and stranger, all at once.
We dance the dance of ages—he and I,
as men and women have, since dawn of time.

The heat of his flesh grafts my body to his.
Listening for his heart, I plead,
"Long and steady, beat!"

My fingers indulge in the silk of his hair.
Inhaling him, I lose myself in the musk of his skin—
drinking him in, flooding my senses, locking
their memories in my heart, preparing my soul:
Take courage! As though he won't be here tomorrow.

How fleeting is time, how precious its graces!
How does one return to living half a life?
I have loved completely into sweet forgetting.

A Thankful Marriage

You said *thank you* to me this morning,
as you traced my body's curves in the gray light.
No, we didn't make love, as we usually do.
We must be getting old.

But still, you thanked me.
For what? I asked.
For everything, you said.
Refresh my memory, I said.

For yesterday — for unpacking a few more boxes, again.
For turning this old house into a beautiful new home,
again. For the wonderful dinner, the awesome dessert,
for staying home with the children and raising them well.
For that quality-of-life moment you snatched from the TV,
reclaiming it on our deck under the summer moon,
with Venus and Mars smiling at the four of us, where
we argued which one was Venus, which one was Mars,
while our son delighted in spying the Big Dipper,
inspiring our daughter to play Bach on her viola.
And you, how you sang "Moon River" with me,
saving it from me, following it with that lullaby
from your Motherland you used to sing to the kids
in their cribs — strange melody in this land: poignant,
bittersweet, like the breeze that caressed our skin
and the leaves as we cuddled on the swing,
which we could have done all night, but didn't.

For I have to leave early this morning to go to work —
again, and leave you to *your* work — here, again,
enduring this tedious, mundane life made rare
and precious only because I have you to share it with.

Thank you for all these, you said.

And I said, *same to you* — for noticing.
I needed it.

At least, that's how I imagined it.

Dream House Hunters

On Sunday mornings when God's houses
        open, my husband and I have a ritual:
We scour the Net for open houses
        plotting noontime's sequel.

These hard times bring both bad and good —
        we're ones not to miss a bargain.
We patiently wait till the clock turns one
        to view the latest showing.

Signs beckon like green grass on the other side,
        promises of dreams still to be lived.
Each façade of brick, stone, or siding — a face,
        welcoming or warning.

Houses are for sale for varied reasons,
        reasons not hard to guess.
As soon as the door opens to greet us,
        the telltale signs are there.

It's the obvious one in the leaflet
        that shyly says "bank-owned."
Maybe the master's closet,
        where hang only a wife's clothes.

Still in another: grand empty rooms —
        mark of an ill-thought purchase?
How could one buy such a big house
        and miss the part where it's furnished?

Estate sales are saddest, still:
        scent of drug-torn bodies;
profiles of shadows on faded wallpaper —
        footprints of untold stories.

Then there's the home with walls that sing
　　　　of a life lived long and well;
　rooms that echo with laughter and tears;
　　　　the kitchen is worn, good vibes dwell.

That's when my husband and I glance at
　　　　each other: *We too have a home like this,*
our eyes seem to say, as we call it a day,
　　　　for our dream, we already live.

For My Daughter and Her Friends
on High School's Eve

What must I tell you — now, that you enter
the spring of your wondrous years?
These ravenous, greedy, curious years,
the playing, teasing, jostling,
and dancing with Life
who is a young buck?

Will you hunt him like Diana — relentless,
and with cunning skill,
yet always with reverence
for life that gives life?

How must you ride him — He,
whose horns have just begun
to grow their fuzz?

Cling jealously to the crowns of Youth,
but when they've shed off their mink,
and they themselves fall off
the wizened head — let them go.
Hang on no more,
lest you too fall with them.
We all grow horns
to lose them to the sage in us.

You are the amazons of your future:
Seize your inheritance and run
with the wind!
Fly like the kites of summer
toward the Morning Star,
yet ne'er too near — lest you burn,
consumed by your own flame.

Hold steadfast to the strings
that bind you to the Earth,
who is your First Mother.

What must I tell you — you,
who look at me with my own eyes of old?
I, who now only yearns to reap
the harvest of my autumn years,
to fill my cornucopia with memories
that feed dreams for winter's slumber?

I tell you: Look around you — always,
with wonder and joy, blessing the Universe
with ceaseless gratitude.

Valentine's Child

How can a mother tell of her deepest secrets —
       of how you came to me on Love's own feast?
I dreamt of you before you came:
       a fragment of heaven, come to honor me.

A cliché indeed it is to say that a mother
       loves the child of her womb;
yet it's Mystery's plot — how a mother
       falls *in* love with her son.

My heart explodes in reckoning with
       the favor of the gods upon me,
       and I am filled with both fear and wonder!
For Narcissus had no beauty like yours:
       While the lad had only a pond of enchantment,
       you have my eyes to look at to
       behold the beauty you possess!

How can I hold you forever, yet
       release you to Destiny's schemes?
I celebrate you with kisses now,
       before time steals you from me,
       before you squirm from my embrace.

Please stay a little longer this way,
       dear fair child of mine:
My electric bundle of sunshine smiles
       and mischievous laughter!

I watch you as you sleep,
       a cherub from Paradise, no less,
Perfection of Perfection itself,
       my dearest love:
Love's own gift!

Bus Boy

"I'll be fine, Mom," he said, this little son of mine,
to persuade me to let him ride the school bus.
All these years, I've been his chauffer,
and now he wants to let me go?
If only I could let go.

My mind surveys scenes of him without me.
My heart races to shield him from would-be bullies.
Visions of school buses throwing off their precious
cargo fill me with dread, let alone hostage
dramas staged off of Innocents' Mile.

My rational mind warns me against paranoia,
only to be taunted by other worries —
I can't bear to think of the possibilities!

Yet there he nonchalantly stands:
Smiling at me with the reassuring smile
of one seemingly strong and wise.
And perhaps he is — as only the young are.
As only the pure-hearted can be.

Though he's only eight to my forty-three,
he could twist my heart into Boy Scout knots
around his little fingers.
And I sigh, resigning myself
to the fate of all mothers:

We can't keep what we hold only in trust.
Birthing, alas, is a long
umbilical cord
of good-byes.

Old Letters

Another move, another house,
not yet a home.
All around me, the scraps and souvenirs
of a life, stuffed in boxes.

How does one measure how far
we've gone on this journey?
Or depth of being?
Or success or failure?

First there were two hundred, then four hundred;
Now eight hundred? Or a thousand, perhaps?
A thousand boxes!
The accumulation of years.

Projects begun but never finished,
vacation snapshots, milestones reached;
The turning at the crossroads,
where the fork stared us in the eye:

Did we choose the road less traveled —
the one that made all the difference?
Or did we, like many, pick the safer path,
rode the bandwagon of mediocrity?

Is this what it all amounts to?
This counting of boxes —
as proof of our lives?
Are we simply then
the sum of a mover's list?

The house is full, yet emptiness
echoes through its rooms.
Until I see them —

the old shoeboxes.
I hesitate—intent cowers at Pandora's curse.
What does the accused plead?
Guilty! Guilty! My accuser screams.
Somewhere, the verdict lies within.

Old letters sing to me—
some old, forgotten melody.
And one by one, they tell my story
in haunting strains of raw symphony.

My mother reaches me across the seas
in the cherished slants and loops of my youth.
I caress the writing as if it were her hand,
as if she were here. I remember them dearly:

These love notes of instructions
for surviving life away from home.
Reminders of family gatherings,
prayers for safety and blessings.

And then—those fateful ones she sent
post my exile to this foreign land.
It was no use, Mama.
There was nothing left for me there.

Half the story lies between the lines;
the other half, here.
Take courage! Keep faith!
Rejoice in second chances.

And from sisters, sweet sisters!
Diaries of parallel lives—
of college things and first loves,
invites for weddings I never witnessed.

So far away from home, so far away.
Can't return home now. Can't.
I wish it were otherwise.
But life's a pretzel, my dears.

And then—the fabric of new life:
in new friends and new places. A new,
loving husband, beautiful children.
Life goes on.

Seasons marked by greeting cards,
hallmarks of celebration and strife.
And in between, the stuff of life:
lamentations on weather and the times.

Gratitude, anger, recrimination;
comic relief, momentous occasion.
Plans, dreams, tedious rhythm of days;
hope and frustration, peace in resignation.

But look here,
yes, here.
Don't you see?

There has always been,
always will be—love.
Precious boxes of life!

My accuser stands silent.

My Mother's Hair

This morning I awoke from a memory
of my mother's hair. I was a mere
child of five — or six?

Lying on my parents' bed, I watched as
Mama unfurled her luxurious black mane
lapping like a thick wave above her waist:

Still slim, unmarred by seven other children
yet to come; still unbent from years
of housework yet to be done.

They smiled at me from the mirror — those
dark, sparkling, slanted eyes of hers, under
bangs that caressed her virgin eyebrows.

She looked like those pretty Asian models
in glossy New Year's calendars given
by Papa's Chinese customers.

Enchanted, I watched as she stroked and
polished every strand, gathered and wove
that silken mass into a smooth, perfect braid,
enticing my small fingers to reach for
Rapunzel's rope — their lifeline to that castle
in the air that promised happy-ever-afters
to girls who brushed tangles off their hair.

But those fingers missed, and I, jolted awake
by fear of falling, reach for a picture of my
mother today, digging up the girl I knew
under cobweb grooves that now line her once
pretty face, beneath crinkled folds now draped

over once sparkling eyes, checking if
that dreamy young mother is still there —
that hopeful bride who'd later shed her royal
veil for a practical salt-and-pepper bob.

And I see that my mother is still a beautiful
woman, undefeated by husband and ten children,
by decades of housework, by years of tears nowhere
visible in these same, old, smiling Asian eyes of hers.

Rapunzel's rope is gone, but so is that castle in the air.

A Letter to My Mother

My dearest Mama,

I smiled — and cried when I read your letter today.
You talked about sending my short story
to the Philippine Palanca Awards.
So much like you to have done that.

All my life you've carried the torch for me —
always pitting me against some new challenge,
lifting me to your higher concept of me.
Yet you never pushed me, and I thank you for that.
Just gave me that right little nudge I needed
to get me started on becoming who I am.
And I love you for that.

Yet they told you I'm not eligible because
I'm no longer Filipino but American now.
The story of my life, isn't it?

Always seemingly caught between worlds —
neither here nor there, neither this nor that,
eluding tidy description, belonging nowhere.

And so they put me in neat little boxes of what I wasn't:
not wealthy or fair-skinned enough, the bourgeoisie said;
not poor or brown-skinned enough, the proletariat said;
not popular or famous enough, the populists said;
not enough of anything, the rest said.

Only you knew who I was before anyone did,
including myself. That's why you named me
after the Lady of Victory, you said — a talisman
against my evil twin, Tribulation.

You knew if I wasn't something of anything,
it was that of someone who'd let others decide
who I am. Such is your mother's love that you still
believe in me. I guess I'll always be your child,
won't I? Like you said, I'll always be your
champion, no matter what anyone says. I wish
I could be as sure of myself as you are.

I'm a mother and a wife, but I also yearn to be
something else — at the same time. What's wrong
with that? To be a writer — yes, a successful writer,
a *New York Times* best seller? Maybe a Pulitzer Prize
winner? (Can you blame me — you, who planted
these dreams in my heart?)

I'd like to be a poet — a people's poet, like Rizal,
Neruda, or Whitman. Remember the first contest
I won? How I recited "O, Captain! My Captain!"?
Did you know Whitman wrote that for Lincoln?

Which reminds me, I wouldn't mind being president
either — to boot out that tough-talking cowboy who calls
those not of his kind "members of the Axis of Evil."
Can you believe that, Mama? As if he knew.

Go ahead — show him, Mama! You, who knows no
night without your litany of prayers, whose knees
are calloused from bent supplication praying for
protection of a son who is also neither here nor there,
neither this nor that, for he's become one of the
invisibles who cook and serve Americans their food,
build their houses, mow their lawns, raise their kids,
clean their homes — yet does not have the right
to be called one of their own.

But I'm not native-born, Mama, you see.

So we can forget the presidency. It's written
in the Constitution — framework of *their*
democracy. Mother *Pilipinas*, too, has
disowned me by law. But how do I
un-become her child just because
I carry the eagle's passport?

I cry for the way the leeches continue to ravage
our homeland. I cry for the failure of leadership
that plagues us like an endless curse. There's nothing
corrupt as political power in Luzviminda's country:
They who drink of it become the insatiable vampires
they've ousted. They do nothing but aggrandize
themselves at the expense of their people.

I cringe at the news aired on international
channels, of how they continue to tear each other
down like the proverbial crabs that won't let
their kind climb up the basket, blind to anything
worth fighting for, together.

This thinking has poisoned our very blood, it seems —
I see its cancer among our *kababayans* here, too.
They'd shoot down their kind if they even suspected
she'd achieve what they couldn't do.
Yes, here in America.

And they wonder why we haven't progressed:
We're quagmired in our own feces!

Yet the dreamer in me still refuses to resign — still
aches to make a difference in this godforsaken world.
Still dreams of advocating for some hopeless cause —
like the cause of our selves. To become once more
the crusading lawyer I'd set out to be, when once
upon a time they allowed me in their exclusive party.

But I can hardly get the laundry done, or the dishes,
or type a word or two between chores, if only to compose
a line for a sorry poem. And they say I'm too old for
anything more. There are so many who are much younger —
born in this country, educated here.

Their kind — not mine, Mama, you see?
I want to ask them what they think *my kind* is.
Can you believe it's the same fight again for me?

Truth is, Mama, I'm tired. I feel old. I wish I knew
who I really am, or what I'm meant to be. I'm no longer
certain, Mama, you see. Not like you — who always
seemed sure of destiny. I want to ask you: Have you
always known who you are, where you belong?

You said you'd always wanted to be a teacher —
so you had children, and became their first mentor.

You said you always wanted to be a mother,
and so you had ten of us. Did you really want all
of us — *all ten* of us, including the one who went
to heaven at three months old because she had
a hole in her heart? Or did you sometimes wish
we didn't come so soon, so many? Did you have
a choice, or did you let your church and husband
decide that for you, too? Were you also tired all
the time, like I am now? And I only have two!

You said you'd always wanted a good husband —
so you stuck it out with a man who didn't drink,
smoke, gamble, or cheat on you. What I want
to know is — did he love you enough, care for you
enough, validate you enough? Did he finally stand
up for you against in-laws who rejected you because
you, too, weren't rich enough, mestiza enough, or

connected enough? Was he good to you
in all the ways you'd hoped a man might be?
Or did he, too, put a hole in your heart?

There are other forms of betrayals, Mama,
you see?

Why you bred in me a fighter yet hardly
fought for yourself confounds me!
Or is it that I missed your point entirely?

Tell me, Mama. I want to know — and in that
knowing, maybe I'll understand:
For myself. For my daughter.
For now. For all time.

Do you have any notion left of me —
to save me?

Your loving daughter.

The Gardener

Bare hands tap root ball out of container,
lower sapling into womb of the earth,
fill the gaps with soil, compacting—
nurturing new life with snug embrace.

He waters around it in gentle cascade,
whispering the mantra of all agents of creation:
This is your place under the sun;
spring forth and be abundant!

Repeating this ritual with remaining brood,
he's oblivious to the aging of the day.
When fading light signals supper's hour,
among progeny, he takes his place.

I watch his hands while he eats, silent.
Dirt still clings under his nails.
I dare not utter my heart's desire:
Papa, speak to me as with your protégées.

Generations

When did we become our mothers,
and our daughters, us?
Youth is a silken thread that shimmers
in the sun, and then is gone.

When did fathers cease to be men,
returned to sons cuddled by mothers;
their memories — frozen in time,
of worlds existing only in the mind?

I have lived long enough to see
that history does not repeat itself —
it repeats us.

Who will break the chains of our past?
Who is worthy of our future?
We seek salvation for ourselves,
finding only derision.

I drink the bitter tea of knowledge,
reaching wisdom in surrender.
I am becoming myself, as I shed myself.

Behold the rebirth, as my children cease
to be their grandparents.

Midwest Winter Garden

North winds blow and sculpt the ghostly terrain.
Winter has cloaked us with its mantle, at
last. As if burying what strives to live
beneath, guarding the buds that spring will bring,
just as we, above, die to start again.

He gazes across the garden, wondering
what birds feast on in their sleep. I watch him
stand before the kitchen window — a grown-
up man now, shadow of the boy I knew.
This frigid, talcum white world fascinates

as much as overwhelms him. I wonder
what emotions churn inside him — does he
feel what I felt when I too had left the
land of our birth and youth? Here we are, now:
siblings, yet more strangers than friends, I fear.

How to catch up with fourteen years gone by?
Like this landscape both old and new, culling
a familiar tune, first forgotten before
remembered in hearts' tentative duet.
Behold, songbirds are feeding on the trees.

To *Lola* on Her Ninetieth Birthday

Beautiful, soft-spoken woman with the timid smile,
crowned with platinum-spun angel's hair: Your
presence in our lives has touched our hearts, for you
never needed trumpets to announce you're there.

Many years ago when I was a child, you
nourished the man whose blood runs in our
veins, and when he was snatched away from
us, you gave him back in a different way.

He was an artist true—a crafter of dreams,
so he left us a fairy with a magic wand who
could spin secret potions for body and soul,
and then some, for broken hearts.

Holidays were merriest with the love
you poured into your legendary hot cocoa.
Now, away from you, on the other side
of the world, I thirst for it.
Do you hear your grandchild's cry?

Were it so my children could be as lucky
to see you work in your magic tower,
where you concoct those special remedies
in the warmth of your kitchen fire.

Ninety years are but a blink in the eye of God,
but for us, an eternity of memories that keep us
grateful for having been blessed with an angel like
you, nudging us always toward our true paths.

May God lend you to us much longer, *Lola*,
for this world makes us old and weary.
Can you brew a special potion to renew

---

our spirits; make us strong, hopeful, merry?

Can you mend the broken ties of our families,
the way you mix different unique ingredients
that taste better because they're together?

We are the ones who are old, as you are forever
young. We search for the fountain of youth,
and find it in wisdom as old as the Earth.

Reconstruction of Lost Things

I don't know what triggered it:
Karen Carpenter singing
"Silver Bells" on the radio,
or the vintage colored light bulbs
strung on a tree in a display window.

I pull over and stop the car,
till I can see the road again.
I want to see, touch, smell,
taste, hear Christmas again!
But where to begin?

First: a galaxy of white lights
around the house; the tree — trimmed
with treasures of Christmases past;
nativity scene — where, they say,
lies the reason for the season;
mistletoe on the ceiling;
wreath on the front door.

In the kitchen: steaming hot cocoa and
apple cider; muffins and cookies rising
in the oven; a flickering cinnamon-scented
candle; a blazing fire; a serenade of carols.

But still I cannot feel it: that magic
that envelops the innocent,
anticipating what's possible,
listening for hooves on the roof.

The neighbors lost their daughter
in a plane crash last summer —
she was my daughter's age.

Around the world, still, children
are starving, women are raped,
men kill and get killed.

All these broken lives —
how does one recover joy?

Not too soon, my son scurries down
the stairs, as my daughter arrives
from college, and my husband's feet
make a sound like thunder as they shake
snow clumps off his boots.

Deep from the well of my gut,
I hear a rumbling not
unlike Old Faithful makes
before it unleashes its gift.

Chapter 5. Journey Through Friendship

BFF

I think of you on cool, sunny mornings,
or quiet, wistful afternoons, or at dusk,
pregnant with the promise of storm —
when solace comes easy
as enjoying a hot cup of tea.

You offered uncommon hospitality
as if it was "no big deal," enough
to make me want to curl upon your
knees like a kitten that had nothing
better to do, nowhere it would rather be,
where I could soak myself in the warm
refuge of license to just be myself,
as if this was all that's expected
of me: laughing as I've never laughed
before, silly as silly gets.

In your company, I've lived some
of the happiest days of my life.

Thank you, my best friend,
forever.

Refugee of Old Dreams

She texts me to say she's at her sister's home
in California, and won't I please call her there.
I'm glad. She didn't sound happy the last time

she emailed, living in her mother-in-law's house
in our hometown on the other side of the Pacific.
Her husband had decided one day to just quit work.

Twenty-five years of toil in the Land of Opportunity
without much to show for it put a toll on his hope,
like it did on hers when she'd realized they'd never

buy a home of their own, nor live the American
Dream. It was easier for them to go back "home,"
he said. She'll welcome having maids at her beck

and call again, he said. But it became clear from
the start that only her mother-in-law had that power.
They were *her* maids, after all, and my friend was

merely a refugee of old dreams. She came close, though.
Couple of years ago, she'd gone back to school to finish
that nursing degree. But her washed-out husband

washed away his own dreams. This wasn't the first time
he'd done this: Pulled her away from hers, just when
they'd come within reach. So, she folded her feelings

and tucked them neatly, as if putting away washed
laundry. Continued on the old path of wives —
following fate and husbands where they pleased.

Tried to pick up where they'd left off in the Motherland,
weaving her life around heirloom patterns. But *it's too hot*

all the time, she cried. Can no longer bear the heat

and humidity oppressive as her nightmares.
Can't breathe, she complained. So, she panted
out hours of rote prayers our mothers taught us,

like some Lamaze breathing exercise. I call her,
but her sister says she's still asleep. Jet lag,
I presume. She came to lend support to a sibling

recovering from hysterectomy. I wonder if she also
returned to excise a cancer of her own: Give caesarian
release to stillborn plans festering in her womb

now reclaiming their long overdue birthday, while
her husband wakes up to his mother barking orders
to the maids, thousands of miles away.

Requiem for a Beloved Friend

Ours was not an everyday friendship,
nor one that makes a weekly call;
time or distance didn't rend our ties,
cemented in principle and squall.

She was old enough to be my mother,
but treated me as her peer and friend;
graced our life with regal presence,
joyful spirit, intelligence.

When crisis came and friendships tried,
she denounced falsehood, vanity, and pride;
rejoiced in blessings, hers and mine:
loving family, friends of the loyal kind;

Above all, the just and righteous, true of
color, meek yet strong—these she admired,
for she was likewise these, and more:
devoted wife, mother, mentor.

You will be missed, Vicky Guadiz--but your
light continues to shine, for your love fired
a torch at the core of our hearts,
and we are grateful ever more.

Kindred Souls

We toil, we weep, our pain seemingly
singular as the affliction of our birth,
our shared curse with Anna Karenina.

But Tolstoy got it wrong.
It is the happy who are unique;
our suffering — our signet
bond as human beings.

Speak softly, caress gently,
oh calming balm of kindred souls,
for life's burdens we must carry,
until eternity reclaims us!

Chapter 6. Journey Through the (Human) Race

People's Poet

You cry to me,
Hope! Hope! Give us hope.
That you'd give anything for a
sputter of meaning to your lives.

I'm sorry to disappoint.
A poet rises no higher
than her source.

For Carson

I didn't know you, nor you, me;
yet I'm inherently drawn to you
by this feeling of losing you, for you
could've been anyone — even my son.

And so I too grieve.

Forgive us for not being there
when you needed a friend.
Forgive us for being somewhere else
when you bid us good-bye.

And so I too say good-bye.

How strange to be saying good-bye
to a stranger — I wish we weren't.
Could there have been something
I could have said, could have done?

And so I too regret.

Truth is, Carson, none of us could have
been good enough, big enough.
For we carried our own burdens close to
our chests, and there was no room for more.

And so I too confess:

I'm not strong, although I wish I were;
I'm not brave, although I wish I were;
I'm not your mother, although I feel I am;
I'm not your keeper; no one is.

Only we are our own keepers — but you weren't
meant to know this until you were strong enough
to know it. We keep such secrets close to our hearts,
you know, and we know it.

This is our tragedy:

To speak when it's too late.
To act when it's too late.
To understand when it's too late.
To love when it's too late.

Abu Graib

They said we did this, this sculpted mass
of twisted bodies. I say, it can't be. Must be
pictures of the Holocaust. Then again—not.
The bodies aren't skeletal.

Still, apocalyptic visions fill the pages,
illuminated by flash photography.
The people aren't dead—yet might as well be.
Where are the olive skins? Wearing only shame,
these ones look pale and cold.

Odd, how temperature is conveyed
by incursions of light. I feel a fever rising
in my soul—what deranged sculptor
imagined this? There he is, with the others—
or is it a she—posing for the camera,
saying cheese?

No, I say, it can't be. They look like children
playing soldiers, perched on their fort
of obscenities. My eyes must be playing
tricks on me. For there, but for the grace
of God, go I. Who knows what
I would've done, in their place?

Nothing corrupts absolutely more than
absolute power, someone said. They proved
it in that psych experiment at some university.
A game of prison guards and prisoners that
ceased to be a game. No one knows when
the line was crossed. Exactly. How would I?

When prisoner and prison guard become
one, I suppose—each a prisoner of his own
momentum of inconsolable fear?

I rub my eyes as I spy myself
in the shadows, smiling,
thumbs up, saying yes
to the camera.

Diaspora of Luzviminda's Children

N.V.M. Gonzalez said,
"How could you return to the homeland,
if you never left it?"

Say this to Luzviminda's children—
scattered o'er the earth, tending to lands
and children of their masters: the engineer
turned oil field worker; the teacher turned
nanny; the nurse turned nursing home aide;
the wife and mother turned housekeeper;
the doctor turned medical clerk; the dancer
turned stripper; the singer turned cook;
the cook turned dish washer; the writer
turned waiter; the accountant turned bank
teller; the lawyer turned paralegal; the
professor turned tutor; the soldier turned
postal worker; the architect turned
construction hand—the best and brightest
of Luzviminda's children, turned into
masses of struggling humanity:
all exiles from Motherland and family.

I see my brother's face on the waiter who
served my dinner; my sister's smile on the
bank teller who processed my check;
my mother's hands on the nanny that
walked her charge in a stroller as I jogged
past them; my father's brow on the gardener
who mows my lawn and clips my hedges.

I see myself in the oil field worker and the nanny;
the nursing home aide and the housekeeper;
the medical clerk and the stripper; the cook

and the dish washer; the waiter and the
bank teller; the paralegal and the tutor;
the postal worker and the construction hand.
I was among the best and brightest of Luzviminda's
children, now wandering in this foreign land:
an exile from Motherland and family.
Yes, I am she and he and the little ones —
all orphaned by this diaspora.

No travesty is greater than of families and nations
interrupted, but we move on, as life always does,
with impunity. We've no time to wallow in misery,
to debate if we're human because we live in the
shadows; whether we're slaves because we do
work others are ashamed to do for slave wages;
whether we're criminals because we've no papers
to show our right to live and work in this land.

Geographical borders are man's creation,
not God's. Life is.

And this is all we want:
To live.

Valentine's Dance of the Mail-Order Bride

She sits, demure, beside her husband — a fat, short man,
at least twenty years her senior. She's draped in polyester
posing as silk — a dark, slinky number trimmed with
plastic gold. She's a pauper queen, but queen
nonetheless to his unrepentant poverty of being.
She's steaming coffee to his chilled milk;
a curious, veiled daffodil peeking
from icy dominion. But she
doesn't look up to meet
our welcome glance.

Shrouded hotel dining table spreads between
us — a bleached ocean proclaiming disparate
worlds, stark division of experience atoned
for by the single red rose standing
at the center: a memorial to
buried secrets, saluting
phoenixes rising
from ashes.

We introduce ourselves to dispel the awkward
moment, saying our names — offering the
labels our mothers gave us to bridge
the distance of our births. Only he says
his name. We don't catch hers.
Or did she?

"Married four months," she says instead, proudly —
the deep, round voice surprising, corners
of lips rising, eyes lifting, checking our
expressions, dipping her fingers in
waters of reception — testing the
warmth, or lack of it.

We congratulate them, and ask how they met. The kiss
of death, if ever a question is, for it pushes her
back to her corner of a hide-and-seek world.
"It's a long story," the husband states,
omitting the story. "Basically met through
another." A compromise. His is no beam
of pride, but measured gauge of rehearsed
line's success. Cryptic breeze swooshes
in gaps of our encounter, threatening
to blow away the few strands of
tendered connections.

"I was nanny for Dubai sheikh's kids. Might
have become his second wife if not for Don,"
she tries, again. We observe the creature
for whom she's exchanged life of sure
luxury — *discount the polygamy!* —
straining to hide our incredulity:
She gave up THAT for HIM?
my husband and I ask each
other with upturned-browed
glance that speak the
unspeakable.

When the emcee announces the Valentine king
and queen, now dancing under gilded cardboard
crowns, our bride returns to her veiled corner,
fortressed by inscrutable eyes, half-smiling
lips, as her husband ignores her urgings
to join the lovers' ritual.

Some rounds on the floor later, my husband
and I retreat to the shadows, glimpsing
the bride in the spotlight — swirling
and swinging to "Dancing Queen"

with the other man-less
women of the night.

She's become Salome in the flesh, while her
husband snores in his corner of dead embers
— bald head nodding unconscious,
momentarily appearing
as if it might
fall off.

Turning a Corner

Let's lick our lips and kiss each other's wounds;
Let's not speak of fear or transgression,
but scent of orange blossoms in the spring.
I want to push the hyacinths to break the ice;
I want to smell the roses sleeping in the bud.

This winter has gone on too long—it's tearing
the skin of my longing apart. What's left is
form of being—slave to the past, jester of hope.
I am not this being. I am not the sum of my parts.

I want to hear the music of children playing
in the streets, but the fat, juicy notes of their
laughter are swallowed by crows preying
from wires burning with groans of dragons
and dungeons in little Pandora's boxes.

My mouth is a cocoon of winged words that can't fly,
stitched shut by silken threads of political correctness.
Are we to be tied down by fear of offense, or bound
by common passion, righteous anger?

Look: The wolves have gone wild with the hunt!
There is the scattered carcass of a nation.
But America is not the sum of its parts!

Call forth the spirit of those turning in their graves,
the souls of those to whom we owe tomorrow.
To the first, say: Remind us of our beginnings.
To the other: Show us a corner to turn around,
together.

Rain-Fool

Ash-gray clouds hang heavy
      over everything, everyone.
Ancient hills are reborn, dressed in rain-fed grass.
They stand like proud breasts of virgins
      arrayed with peridots,
pushing against pregnant sky.

The sun is fighting for remembrance
      behind the aged scalp of heaven —
a formless light peeking between
      gaps of precipitation,
ending as vague halo
      'round a dead saint's head.
It hasn't rained this much in California
      in a hundred years.

God knows this place needs the water,
      but mudslide-weary homeowners curse it.
It's nothing more than Nature
      reclaiming its destiny.

Man fighting Nature is a fool.
      Man denying Nature
is a big, dead fool.

One doesn't build a house
      on shifting sands
and expect everyone to pay for it.
      This is, after all, desert land.
There's a wise parable on that.

Paradise left for vacation —
      resting from our spoiled demands.

We're only its caretakers, after all—
        accent on the *care*,
not the *take*.

It's the height of arrogance
        to whine about the weather.
You've got to take
        the bad with the good.

Embrace it, rest easy
        in shelter built on rock,
surrendering to hypnotic mantra
        of rain-drums on roof,
irrigating us with fertile dreams of young
        virgins dancing with Dionysus.

Pilgrim II

The certificate arrived in the mail.
I'm now a child of Uncle Sam.
Many years of toil culminate in this:
    a remnant of dead trees.

I look at the badge of my new allegiance,
    feeling strange lack for my betrayal.
I ask myself what this paper has given.
The answer eludes me: the ultimate irony.

Surely not freedom: it comes with a price in this land;
Surely not equality: it applies mostly to white men;
Surely not social security: there's hardly any, nowadays;
Surely not safety: these are dangerous times for the
        U S of A;
Surely not the American Dream: many are trapped
    in its nightmares;
And surely *not* the surety of union with my Beloved:
    for sometimes, love is not enough.

What, then, have I sacrificed loyalties for,
    in foregoing with patriotic schemes?
In leaving one's Motherland — and with her,
    my childhood dreams?
What life have I bartered for hard-earned
    vocation, forsaken?
What joys of the heart gained, in place
    of family abandoned?

Pray, tell me, Uncle Sam!

For I'm the same as ever before:
I'm no freer: true liberty comes
    from freedom of the mind;

I'm no more equal to any man: equality comes
        from humanity's soul;
I'm no more secure: this is the gift of faith and hope;
I'm no more the dreamer: my dreams
        transcend political boundaries;
I'm no less vulnerable to love's loss:
        for Love, alas, is its own master —
        it comes and goes as it pleases.

I'm a traveler in search of new frontiers, and I find:
The only ones left are those in my mind.

And don't even bother with outer space.
The generals of capitalism have rocket-launched
        its schisms beyond this planet.
I wonder if anti-globalists see
        their fight has become obsolete?

And now, what's this?
        To spread democratic bliss?
Don't you know you can't make a people free, unless,
        with *their own blood*, they pay for it?

One of your great sons said:
Ask not what your country can do for you,
but what you can do for your country.

That was nice, back then. But today we say:
No more — to human sacrifices before altars
        of corporate gods and states!
No more — to paying the king's ransom; rather,
        ransom the people's fate!

And oh, by the way,
I don't mean it in the way
totalitarian Communism does.

Nor even Fascism, disguised as moralism.
Nor radical religiosity —
    that dark den of bigotry.
For these too have bared their ugly heads to us:
They're as frightful as the monsters
    they seek to oust!

Call me left wing, right wing, or reactionary —
    as you please.
But I call the shots here — here, in my mind.
I don't have to submit to an ideologue's world.

Truth is: Peoples are real; states are not.
Human life, priceless; greed, insatiable.

Geographical borders are contrived walls against
    our failure to hug humanity as one.
Thus, we continue to walk the earth as wandering
    strangers, never arriving home.

Despite it all, I am grateful, Uncle Sam,
    for indeed one thing is true:
This is the one place on Earth I can say these
    things to someone like you
    (and still keep my head)!

For better or worse, you are now my home;
    and your people — mine, too.
I first came to you for love of a man;
    now I stay for the love of mankind.

For in this fight for stubborn dreams, this arena,
    for now, is as good as it gets.
I may sound apologetic, yes, but
    I assure you, I will not rest,

till your boundaries are divest
  of old precincts,
and you truly become—

Land of the Free!

Rattled in Seattle

Morning crashes the windows
of my daughter's apartment
in the rattle and din of recyclables
being dumped in collection bins,
the groaning, belching lurch and heave
of buses transporting their day's
portion of travelers, the alternating
angry yells of the miserable
and the chirpy chatter of the hopeful.

The constant ebb and flow of a city
that is alive wash over me like a
simultaneous rising and receding
tide: I am the passive voyager floating
where they take me, receiving without
judging the proof of parallel lives:
both a cacophony of the dead
and symphony of the living.

Should I dive in and throw myself
into this exercise yet again?
I have lived long enough to know
it doesn't end, doesn't care—
this unrelenting march of life,
toward where, I'm still not sure.

I am content to stay in pause
for now, while others push play
into their crescendo of dreams,
wondering if they'll hit the high notes.

The Dying Season

A mortician said it starts in September,
goes on till March, follows the trail of
the flu season: the fall leading a funereal
march into the deep winter of our mourning.

A friend's death seemed to trigger it—
soon, same news of someone's father,
another's mother, an old, friendly waitress,
a turned cop, celebrities and their girlfriends;
children killed by gun and gang violence;
mass murders in Syria, Mali, Libya, Iraq;
the teen suicides of Iowa; genocides in
Somalia, Bosnia, Cambodia, Auschwitz,
and those of the unforgotten Armenians—
inviting a meteor to crash upon this earth,
as if obliging our collective death wish.

Grief washes over humanity, yet
weary hearts fail to weep.
They said *tears are for the living;*
hope, for the livid.

I try to say *I love you* to family and friends
each day, a magic spell to shield them
from harm along their way. Yet death
is the great equalizer—rudely oblivious
to the worth of our dreams: each life
that succumbs carries with it the trash
and treasures of our schemes.

I look at myself in the mirror and ask,
Who am I in all of this?
A blurry image replies,
It is I who lives. Who lives!

Chapter 7. Journey Through the Soul

Breakthrough

One night, one journey, on the dead sea of night:
In search of, yearning for the joy of life.

The Spirit moves in me, longing to be released,
Oh, my soul, when will you find peace?

Something tells me, *got to let it go.*
Got to break down barriers in this brooding ego.

Over the past, in ceaseless haunting,
Day and night, always taunting.

Got to have courage, got to be strong.
Never should quit, have to be reborn.

This is the day when I conquer the night;
This is the moment I begin to fight.

You can freely choose which life to lead;
But you've got to lose the doubts that you live.

You can make the decision — right here and now;
So break the illusions of your chains, somehow.

At the end of the day, when your time is near,
You can move on and say, "It was worth it, my dear."

Meditations Before a Sink Full of Dirty Dishes

Where I came from,
someone else had this job.
Where I came from,
someone was always poorer than you —
no matter how poor you were.
Interesting how human society is built
upon a hierarchy of slaves — yes, even
here in America. No one is exempt:
someone is always lording over us.
More so at the top — where
strings are tighter, trickier.

There's something both repulsive
and attractive in washing dishes.
Repulsive: the chaotic mingling
of disparate flavors, textures, smells.
Attractive: bringing order out of
disorder, the way the pile of colorful,
dirty dishes looks like sculpture: a
promise of new beginnings, of how
good things can still become.

There's still beauty waiting to be seen;
poetry waiting to be heard.

I see and hear: The sparkle and tinkling
music of water pouring like liquid
diamond upon the messy remains of our
consumption. Making it all shine again.

There's something humbling and liberating
in manual labor, menial task — in washing
dishes with bare hands: warm caress of
cascading water; silk embrace of velvet soap;

playfulness of bubbles; finality of glass;
strange pleasure of cold steel; primal beat
and rhythm of hand, water, and china dancing
in mantraic choreography that roots you in the
moment. Gives you raisin fingers, shedding
the soul of trappings — binding it naked
to the rawness of living.

God is in the quotidian
details of our lives.

Easter Vigil

And what more do I have to give?
I am tired and sucked dry;
blood oozes out of these fingers
in place of words that would not come.

Fly me to my Muses
out there, in the western realm,
then far beyond, into the south-east
corridors of time.

Revive me with the songs of my youth,
the ones left out to petrify in
winds of rumored obsolescence —
this heart is ancient, not antiquated.

Let me gather the colors of my rainbow,
erect a ladder to redemption —
this mind is ripe for the harvest,
this body poised for resurrection.

I realize now: This time is not
the time to give,
but to receive.

Mark of Life

And so, Life: Here I am.
An unmistakable punctuation in your book.
When will you answer the question mark
                         staring at you?

And while we're on this subject,
what say you to the exclamation point
of your excesses?
                         Your sins of omission!

I've lived half a lifetime with you – and
I'm tired of being a comma
on your page, a breath of silence
                         on the brink of discovery,
yet never getting there.

When will you transform me into a colon –
and make way for my destiny?
Or will you yet again
                         put me on pause:
a semi to *ad infinitum*?

There's nothing left to say.

So while you keep mum on your designs,
I think I'll stick around here awhile –
an ellipsis to your thoughts,
                         hanging in there…

Till I become a period – as black, final and resolute
as Poe's raven to my sentence –
no more run-ons with Fate,
                         no regrets, no despair.

Stamping the irrefutable proof
of my existence—mute witness
to the writing on the wall—
                    decapitated head of a queen
  crying, *I was here!*

I was here.

The Purity of Nothingness

There's a place in me where no one goes but I.
That I've kept only for myself — that not even
my husband or parents or friends know,
or that my children could drink up dry,
or that small-minded people
could destroy.

In that place, I've stashed dreams not even I know
all by name, whose password always changes,
so that no one can steal them when I'm not
looking, or when I'm asleep and only
nightmares visit.

Yet to me they're always there — in a song,
a poem, a look, or a smile, in a scent or
a rainbow, or a touch that burns
invisible scars to life — throbbing,
wounding all over again, till
I taste the salt of forgiveness
and settle score with myself:
"What have you done
with your life?"

And I am shamefully proud to admit
I have done nothing worthy
of monuments.

My footprints on this earth are
already being blown
away by the wind
as I speak.

This is the purity of
nothingness.

The Sleepers

I woke up one day in a house where everyone
was sleeping. I went from room to room, shaking

them, but they complained and stayed in the comfort
of their beds, snoring, refusing to open their eyes.

I drew up the blinds, opened the windows,
letting ribbons of celestial light float in with

the cool morning air, revealing fairy dust dancing
in angels' rays. Yet still everyone remained

sleeping, cocooning themselves more tightly
in their dreams and nightmares, unwilling

to surrender to the new day. So I opened the door
and stepped outside, and I, with my new skin and bare

feet, hugged the ground with its sweet-sour smell
of damp earth and rotting things,

curing my senses with the balm of compassion.
And I followed the maya's song,

as it left clues on branch to branch, its call
echoing in the empty valleys,

scraping the cliffs with its melody.
Till I reached the peak of Mount Olympus.

And I realized: This is where the gods go
while waiting for the sleepers to wake up.

In the meantime, I heard the sound

of children playing.

And I realized: The gods are none other
than children waiting no longer to play.

Thus, I caught the ball of Time
eagerly in my hands.

Messenger

Messenger, thou art damned.
You have betrayed
your trust in my Word.
You have wedged yourself
between my Beloved and me.
It is you who is the false prophet.

How long shall I have to wait
for the faithful one?
How long until night clothes me
with stars? Until day showers me
with dawn, blessing me
with the sunset of my years?

I am a voice crying in the wilderness —
no one hears me. I am a desert rose —
no one sees me. Except the scorpion
passing me by — snickering,
telling me that dust is my fate.

Messenger, your false notes sting
the air with hapless tunes.
You have robbed the hungry
of their ears — so now they can't feed
their souls with my songs.

Woe to you — for you have brought
the wrath of your destiny upon yourself.
You are cursed like many others before
you — setting yourself to be flung down
your mountain, begging for the life
you've squandered on your vanity.

Better to be a rose blooming under

the desert sun, where rabbits feast
on its nectar, delivering it up to the
hawks that kiss the sky.

Yet woe to the flame that blinds
all who see it; that burns
all who touch it.

Contemplations

What now, cryptic Life?
What's real only exists in dreams.
What's true only is heard in silence.
Am I cursed to hunt the elusive?
My pen is mute.

Who hears me?
Who reads me?
Am I but a mote in the eye of God?
Am I but a figment of my imagination?

Something is either dying or fighting in me —
        hanging on, struggling against surrender.
As long as I am restless,
        I know I am alive.

Yet what's the worth of one life?
Is it but a feather plucked from an angel's wing?
A strand of hair falling — unknown,
        from the scalp of God?

By what field is greatness measured?
Is it wealth, or fame, or power?
Or fidelity, even to menial task?
I think the latter.
But how does it matter?

Amazing are the stories we weave
        into security blankets — to lend
        meaning to our lives — to shield
        us from our failures.

Even God, we create in our own image,
	and then call him God,
	or Yahweh, or Allah, or Jesus,
	and then draft him into our wars.

Which leads me to wonder:
Is God then a mere figment
	of our imagination?
What incredible gods
	we've evolved!

In the end, it's imagination that saves us:
	survival of the fittest deity.
Darwin was right.

Exorcism of Childhood Saints

Why do you stare at me with blank eyes, you
whitewashed, broken idols of centuries past,
bought for pennies on the dollar at some antique
auction? What do you say to me now, you mute
legacies of some colonial ruler?

What prayers did you hear in vain from the lips
of the oppressed, those that suffered their souls
for a piece of paradise promised, then stolen by the
white man — that self-anointed savior of our souls?

I pray, spare me from your odious charm — that
opium of the mind that makes mankind blind to
man's inhumanity to man, all in the name of God.
I pray, be gone, Satan!

What salvation did you offer to the desperate;
the sick of mind, body, soul; the innocents sacrificed
to your priests? I pray, be gone, Satan — lest I toss
you into the sanctifying fires of my temple, and
there, to ashes remain forever!

Let the evil spirits be cleansed from you, that you
may whisper to me the hopes of the afflicted, the
voices of the forgotten, the yearnings of souls that
still roam the Earth, seeking freedom from the
shackles of their forced baptism.

Now I see the compassionate Lady among you —
the Mother of us all, the female god-nature denied
by men inherent in our dreams of "god-in-us."
Behold the humble Master among you — who
preached that love is the only true religion.

Let us pray together.
And be at peace.

Quantum Entanglement

I stand on the precipice of knowing everything and
then, nothing. What shall I gain if I ventured to leap?
Some lost memory of myself in a parallel world?

Scientists say poets speak their language when
they sing, "We are made of stardust, no less."

Einstein proposed that all matter broke from its half
in the Big Bang, yet forever linked by a string of energy,
so that change in one caused change in the other.

All this time we've been looking for what we lacked,
tried to fill that void with a god, lover, or some other
addiction, not knowing that what we pined for
was none other than our selves.

Perhaps my half leaped on the other side of the universe,
pulled me into the mathematical equation of my destiny.
Here, I ask why, not realizing I myself made that choice.

Yul said, *it's a puzzlement.*
No more?

After Dust Settles

I sit before my kitchen table sipping morning
coffee, as walls shake and floor trembles,
jackhammers at work already.

Dust covers everything — each surface, nook,
and cranny — none escapes its omnipresence,
filling nostrils, filming beverage.

I am breathing it, drinking it — I'm breathing and
drinking this old house: my home now that was home
to others, ingesting also the shadows of their lives?

I examine my skin, note the throb on my wrist, feeling
for sensation of past lives swimming inside me.
This house is going to be the death of me.
The life of me. The mark of me.

I feel I have forever been chasing a sense of being
from a sense of place buried deep inside me — a
forgotten memory etched in the folds of my brain:
a scar from some fight with Fate that won't fade?

How can one explain how brick and stone and
wood can speak to you, whisper secret designs
of rebirth? This house is renovating me as much
as I am it: we are, together, evolving into each other.

I walk around the rooms and see what they were,
what they are becoming — and I hear the sound of
living that dwelt in them; the sound of music that
will fill the air, instead of dust, after dust settles.

After dust settles, I'm going to pick myself up where
I dropped myself off before this house possessed me.

After dust settles, I'm going to edit the excesses
of my life out of this home, prevailing over
the dust of my life.

After dust settles.

Memory of Water

I. An hour before sundown, on the cusp of spring:
water cascading over rocks upon man-made
pond teeming with fish my husband bought

from the pet shop for twenty-five cents a piece.
I fear the mallard ducks and cranes will fly
overhead and remembering, stop over this oasis

to feed upon my husband's fish. Is this why
they call them "feeder fish"? And why we don't
put koi: costs an arm and a leg— much more than

the price of human life, these days. It's our species
that kills its kind for nothing. "Have you seen
my goldfish?" my husband asked.

How a grown man could delight in such little
creatures. I wonder whether he sheds secret
tears for the ones the brown female mallard ate?

But I remember how an emerald-collared male rode
her the other day, marking and mucking the water
with their lovemaking. I wonder how the fish

could stand such obscenity! Yet why do we feel
repulsed by life repeating itself? The female must
be preparing to return what she took. Life for life:

that's how the cycle goes. How could I—a mother—then
condemn her? She swims, feasting, unmolested, beak-
diving for the fish my husband will replace, without tears.

II. What, in the sound of water, do we find soothing?
Scientists say that's where we came from: amphibians

145

that learned to walk and live on dry land.

We've lived so long on this land, we've forgotten
our beginnings. Yet with trickling, splashing, flowing
music, fetal memory returns with memory of water:

our first womb. It's the sea — not the earth that birthed us.
The second only swallows us on the voyage home.
One hour before day closes shop: the twilight hour

before half a life is gone, before the second half begins.
Where has the first half strayed? We are worn down,
rock-bare — our rough edges eroded like river stones,

leveled smooth to our lowest common denominator
by the slow, sure, sculpting force of the river of life.
How then shall we face the second half of our lives?

Naked and disarmed, we've been reduced to helpless new-
borns, yet deprived of luxury of time, strength of youth.
With what sharp and fearsome weapons shall we fend off

the enemies still to come? Even our horns have been
ground down to our skulls — not even the stubs remain.
Too tired to fight anymore. No need to fight anymore.

At the right angle and speed, we fling ourselves upon
the river's surface and bounce-skip to the other side.
Faith is the shoe that enables us to walk on water,

or become pebbles of resignation — diving into our fates,
mothering ripples of change. Everything has a purpose
in this world — yes, even this pebble.

Isn't this what Fellini's fool said in *La Strada*?

———

146

These Are The Rains

These are the rains that bring autumn's colors,
inspire nesting and snuggling,
leak pause of good breath.

These are also the rains that bring the gray,
flood homes and cities,
drown children and crops.

Everywhere, nature is at work —
for us, against us;
knows no master,
but the force of itself.

We are the ones who give
meaning to the seasons;
and in this, we are
invincible.

Epilogue

Homecoming

Come back with me
to where cicadas smother the dusk
with their mating song, rousing
Dama de Noche from her nap, soaking
the night air with her seduction.

There, the stars shine like watchful eyes
in labyrinthine onyx sky,
and the warm breeze caresses
like a lover's fevered hands.

Do you remember how
we listened to the ocean
inside Neptune's ears?

Oh, how I long to see the moon —
a gold medallion etched
with Madonna and Child,
rising to jubilant arms
of coconut trees waving and singing,
"Hallelujah! Hallelujah!"

There, I remember how the Goddess paints
a ribbon of magic upon gentle tides, paving
the shimmering path for sweethearts' *bancas*
kissing the waters with prayers of adoration.

I can hear the *gitaras* strumming the melancholy
notes of *haranas*, haunting the evening
with serenades passed on by generations
of troubadours — the voices of suitors
forever yearning for lost loves.

How long before the exile returns

to the Birthland?
Shall I live the salmon's fate—
banished to foreign waters
until death calls?

Alas, only time sweetened
by love's memory has
the power to build
bridges burned
back to life.

Acknowledgements

I thank the very talented artist, Miss Nicole Dana, for the beautiful, soulful painting she created as cover design for this book, her clever illustrations for the chapter headings, and our enjoyable, creative collaboration.

I am also grateful for the support and helpful critiques and suggestions provided by my friends and fellow poets in the Omega Poetry Group and the Iowa Poetry Association.

I am especially thankful to the following members of my family and my early mentors who provided me with the tools by which to dream and achieve what other writers and poets have accomplished — to write and be heard:
      –my mother, Mrs. Teresita A. Grageda, for nudging me from an early age to face and rise to the challenges and opportunities the world presents;
      –my father, Mr. Jose L. Grageda, for humoring my curious young mind, introducing me to the smart use of the thesaurus, and teaching me the persuasive value of a well-written composition;
      –my aunt, Miss Zenaida Arcilla, who introduced me to the wonderful world of books and thus a vision of an extraordinary life;
      –my high school writing, literature, and English teachers — Mrs. Anne Gueco (who is also my beloved aunt), Mrs. Mirasol Ajos, and Ms. Marilyn Gueco — who opened my mind and soul to the amazing world of literature and the transformative power of the written word;
      –my children, Francesca and Travis, for tolerating my dragging them into poetry readings with "old people" and putting up with my fickle housekeeping so I may realize dreams in addition to the privilege of being their Mom, and;
      –my husband, Steve, for his generous gift of time,

space, and resources so I may indulge in the luxury of creative freedom.

Last but not least, I am indebted to Ms. Veronica Leighton, editor and publisher of VIA Times, and the following other publishers of my individual poems who, through their kind patronage and support inspired me to forge ahead with this bigger dream of publishing this collection:

Pilgrim I, published as *Pilgrim* in *Dicta*, the literary journal of the University of Michigan School of Law, 1995, and *VIA Times*, July 2011

Warrior Heart, published in *In the Spotlight Magazine*, summer 2004, and *VIA Times*, August 2011

To the WASPy Old Gentleman Across the Room, published as *To an Elder California Gentleman* in *In the Spotlight* magazine, summer 2004

Dancer, published in *In the Spotlight* magazine, winter 2005 and *VIA Times*, May 2013

Sculptor, published in *In the Spotlight* magazine, winter 2005

Second Time Around, published in *Lyrical Iowa*, 2008, and *VIA Times*, February 2012

Journey, published by the 2009 Des Moines Regional Transit Authority (DART) "Poetry in the Buses" Project, and *VIA Times*, October 2012

A Love Letter to My Students, published in *Lyrical Iowa*, 2010

Homecoming, published in *VIA Times*, June 2011

For My Daughter and Her Friends on High School's Eve, published in *VIA Times,* September 2011

My Mother's Hair, published in *VIA Times,* October 2011

The Gardener, published in *VIA Times,* November 2011

Reconstruction of Lost Things, published in *VIA Times,* December 2011

Messenger, published in *VIA Times,* January 2012, and *Lahi,* the Filipino-American Association of Iowa (FAAI) newsletter, January 2012

Easter Vigil, published in *VIA Times,* March 2012

Turning a Corner, published as *Turning Around a Corner* in *VIA Times,* April 2012

Rain-Fool, published in *VIA Times,* May 2012

Mark of Life, published as *A Mark of Life* in *VIA Times,* June 2012

Fossils in July, published in *VIA Times,* July 2012

A Love Song for My Husband, published in *VIA Times,* August 2012

After Dust Settles, published in *VIA Times,* September 2012

A Thankful Marriage, published in *VIA Times,* November 2012

Diaspora of Luzviminda's Children, published in *VIA Times,* December 2012

Breakthrough, published in *VIA Times*, January 2013

Valentine's Dance of the Mail-Order Bride, published in *VIA Times*, February 2013

Contemplations, published in *VIA Times*, March 2013

The Sleepers, published in *VIA Times*, April 2013

Dancer, published in *VIA Times*, May 2013

Sculptor, published in *VIA Times*, June 2013

Singer, published in *VIA Times*, July 2013.

Musician, published in *VIA Times*, August 2013

Painter, published in *VIA Times*, September 2013

A Letter to My Mother, published *in VIA Times*, October 2013

Sunset on a Beach on the Other Side of the Pacific, published in *VIA Times*, November 2013

About The Author

Maria Victoria A. Grageda-Smith was born in Angeles City, Philippines, the eldest of ten children in a family of modest means. Through full academic merit scholarships and the application of talent and industry, she overcame the poverty that continues to plague many of her Third World countrymen and prevents them from having many viable life options. After graduating among the top students of her pre-law and law degree programs from the University of the Philippines, she practiced law as associate attorney in one of the largest law firms in Manila and later became the sole female counsel to one of the largest global companies in Southeast Asia before she met and married her American husband and moved to the United States of America.

After immigrating to the United States, she attended the University of Michigan Law School where she attained her master of laws degree. Later, she found that the frequent travel required of her husband by his career, in addition to the challenges of a mixed-culture marriage, plus the responsibility of raising her children absent the usual support of her network of Philippine family and friends were compelling reasons that necessitated a radical reinvention of vocation, leading her to choose to be the at-home parent. At the same time, her desire to apply herself to creative endeavor that did not require her to work away from home led her to rediscover and pursue a childhood passion: writing poetry and fiction. In this regard, her Philippine heritage and law practice years, her immigrant experience, and her family's travels abroad and frequent moves across the United States in support of her husband's career combine to lend her a unique perspective that informs and inspires her writing.

Today, she writes a monthly poetry column for a Chicago-based immigrant newsmagazine, *VIA Times*. Her poetry has been published in, among others, *Lyrical Iowa*; *Dicta* (the University of Michigan Law School literary journal); and other arts and literary publications. She founded and ran a poetry program for the Iowa Homeless Youth Shelters from 2007 to 2009. In 2002, she was chosen as a featured poet at the Austin International Poetry Festival. She continues to read and perform her poetry in a variety of poetry readings and festivals.

Her fiction gained national US recognition when her short story *Portrait of the Other Lady* won first place in a nationwide short story contest. The short story and an interview of her were published in a Los Angeles-area newspaper (*Portrait of an Award-Winning Short-Story Contest Winner, Ventura County Star Sunday Arts & Living* edition, November 28, 2004). She was selected as a participant in the 2005 UCLA Asian-American Writer's Program and in the same year was interviewed and featured as an up-and-coming Asian-American writer in several media articles (*Finding Their Voice, Philippine News* [Los Angeles area newspaper edition], July 6–12, 2006; *Light in the Shadows*, Philippinenews.com [San Francisco-based online edition], May 18, 2005).

In pursuing her writing vocation, Ms. Grageda-Smith also served as officer of various writers' clubs, conducted writing workshops, and managed her own critique guilds. She is a member of the Iowa Poetry Association and the Des Moines-based poetry critique group Omega. In November 2013, the Chicago Filipino American Hall of Fame honored her with the "Outstanding Writer and Community Volunteer Award."

Warrior Heart, Pilgrim Soul: An Immigrant's Journey is her first book of poems. This collection chronicles the inherently conflicted yet ultimately rich, textured, and hopeful journey of an immigrant woman compelled to confront and achieve a revolutionary redefinition of individual and national identity against a backdrop of life-changing circumstances and parallel historical developments in the United States and the world.

Made in the USA
San Bernardino, CA
01 March 2014